GLADYS FAMORITO

BOUNCE BACK!

How to survive, thrive and maximise
your challenging life situations

GF
BOOKS

First published in Great Britain in 2015
By GF Books – Changing lives through words
Tel: +44 (0) 870 750 1969
www.gladysfbooks.com

1 3 5 7 9 10 8 6 4 2

© 2015 Gladys Famoriyo

All rights reserved. No part of this book may be transmitted or reproduced in any form by any means without permission in writing from the publisher.

Printed and bound in Great Britain by
Berforts Information Press

Book cover design: Tash Webber (www.tashwebber.com)

Typeset in Sabon

ISBN 978-0-9926195-2-7

Scripture quotations marked (NTL) are taken from the Holy Bible, New Living Translation, © 1996, 2004, 2007 by Tyndale House Foundation. Used by permission of Tyndale House Publishers, Inc., Carol Stream, Illinois 60188. All rights reserved.

Scripture quotations marked (NKJV™) are taken from the New King James Version®. Copyright © 1982 by Thomas Nelson, Inc. Used by permission. All rights reserved.

Scripture quotations marked (MSG) are taken from The Message, copyright © Eugene H. Peterson. Published by Nav Press, Colorado Springs, Colorado, in association with Alive Communications, Colorado Springs, Colorado. Permission sought.

Scripture quotations marked (AMP) are taken from the Amplified Bible, copyright © 1954, 1958, 1962, 1964, 1965, 1987 by The Lockman Foundation. Used by permission.

Praise for *Bounce Back!*

Everyone faces times in their life when they experience trouble and distress. We are hit, often unavoidably, by the stuff of life. It can shake us, hurt us, and at times knock us down and out. However, with help, we can learn ways to stand up to these challenges and deal with these encounters. By doing so, we can bounce back and overcome the effect, turning it into a means to move forward. This book aims to give the insight and resources to equip us to respond to the bombardment of life events and to move forward with God's help.

Jonathan Clark – Director for Premier Lifeline

This book is a must-read! It is an essential guide along the journey of life's challenges and adversities. Gladys writes with passion and encouragement to call us higher, to go further, to become more than overcomers, in and through Christ.

Arianna Walker – author, speaker and Executive Director of Mercy UK

Bounce Back! is an amazing book of practical steps to bounce back when adversity hits in life. Gladys has combined compelling life stories, humour and spirituality to make this book a must have and must read for everyone. The simplicity of the book makes it an easy read despite the depth and the richness of the content. I recommend this book for personal use and a resource for schools and churches.

Yemi Adedeji – Associate Director with Hope UK. Ambassador for Compassion UK and Cinnamon Network. Director for 'One People Commission' at Evangelical Alliance UK

Impactful and life changing! A truly inspirational and comprehensive guide on how to emerge triumphantly from life's traumas and setbacks. This 'must have' book will not only equip you with the tools to develop resiliency in the face of challenges, but also how you can become better in the process. Sharing life strategy tools and uplifting testimonials of individuals who have 'bounced back', Gladys skilfully takes the reader on a journey to wholeness and purpose.

Sharon Platt-McDonald – Director for Health, Women's Ministries and Disability Awareness for the Seventh-day Adventist churches in the UK and Ireland.

GLADYS FAMORIYO

BOUNCE BACK!

Contents

Acknowledgements	xiii
Preface	xv
How to Use this Book	xxi
The Journey	xxv
Introduction	xxvii

Part I – Surviving — 1

Chapter One: What Doesn't Kill Us ... — 3

Flip adversity and trauma on its head	4
Use your life's dramas as a catalyst for positive change	6
Victim or victor? You choose!	10
Reflective Questions	11

Chapter Two: Curb the Spiritual Fits and Holy Tantrums — 13

The day I yelled at God	14
When bad things happen to good people	18
Don't throw in the towel	21
Reflective Questions	26

Chapter Three: Handling Life's Unscripted Moments — 27

    When calamity strikes, press on — 28
    Keep digging for gold — 31
    Avoid the blame game — 34
    Reflective Questions — 39

Part II – Thriving — 41

Chapter Four: Maximise your Downtime — 43

    Embrace your seasons — 43
    Stop fighting change! — 47
    Don't let your 'issues' rob you of your potential to be great — 50
    Reflective Questions — 55

Chapter Five: Get Back in the Saddle — 57

    Change your perspectives — 57
    Adapt to your seasons — 62
    Adopt godly strategies — 65
    Reflective Questions — 68

Chapter Six: Develop a Bounce Back Hero Mindset — 71

    Keep hope alive — 71
    Move beyond the pain — 77
    If your dream is big enough, the facts simply don't count! — 85
    Reflective Questions — 91

Part III – Maximising — 93

Chapter Seven: Don't Waste Your Pain! — 95
- Maximise your waiting room experience — 96
- Feel the pain but do it anyway! — 102
- Listen to your life! — 109
- Reflective Questions — 113

Chapter Eight: Reinvent Your Purpose — 115
- Create a meaning for your life — 116
- Arise and shine … your purpose awaits! — 120
- Become unstoppable — 126
- Reflective Questions — 134

Chapter Nine: Now, Pay It Forward! — 135
- The Ten Principles of Bouncing Back — 136
- Have a clear mission — 138
- Make it happen — 145
- Get the support and resources you need — 148

Conclusion: Finishing Well — 157

Take the Bounce Back Pledge — 161

Discover More Bounce Back! Resources — 165

Start Paying It Forward Today! — 167

About The Author — 169

Also Available from the Author — 171

Quit Hiding, Start Living! — 173

Healing a Discouraged Heart — 177

Overcoming Emotional Baggage — 179

The Overcoming Emotional Baggage for Women Initiative — 181

Further support — 183

My Notes — 187

Dedication

I would like to dedicate this book to all the children sponsored by Compassion UK, including my own sponsored children, Aster and Jyoti, who, despite poverty, are choosing to bounce back everyday with Jesus by their side.

Acknowledgements

Thank you Father for another opportunity to write. I would like to say a special thank you to my Mum, Prophetess Joyce Famoriyo, for your unwavering love, support and encouragement. Thank you for all the calls and texts that came just at the right time. I deeply appreciate all your prayers including your daily 'all night' intercessions through the years. I am truly blessed to have the world's best Mum.

To my dear Pastor Agu Irukwu, thank you for all your efforts to see your spiritual children maximise their God-given potential. A true pastor with a father's heart. You always speak words of wisdom and life so we can be all God wants us to be. You are truly appreciated.

To my mentor/big 'bro' and the most dapper Canon I know, Yemi Adedeji. Thank you for always being there and inspiring me to reach for higher.

To the late Dr Myles Munroe, your legacy has propelled me to maximise my potential and stay on track with my purpose. You are a giant on whose shoulders I dare to stand.

To my dear friends (you know who you are) who have laughed, cried, prayed and celebrated with me, I thank God for your lives. You have truly made a positive difference to my journey. I cannot imagine travelling this road without you. You are the best.

To my awesome publishing team – Wanda ('manuscript doctor'), Tash (your creativity knows no ends), Jacqui, Nicky and Theresa – Thank you for helping me make this a reality.

To the Compassion UK team, including Hayley H, Hayley M, Natasha, John and the rest of the crew, I salute you all. Thanks for your labours of love.

Preface

For years, I have been intrigued as to what makes some people appear to recover better than others after adversity, trauma or a challenging life situation. Why is it that some experience positive changes in their outlook? How come they appear grow as a result of their situation and go on to transform the course of their lives? I don't believe this is because they have superhero powers, nor is it that they have nerves of steel. Yet they seem enabled to carry on with life, and often go on to do things they perhaps might not have done had the 'experience' not happened.

In studying such lives and that of my own, I am convinced, without a shadow of doubt, that something positive can come out of our life dramas. In his book, *When Bad Things Happen to Good People*, Harold Kushner, following the death of his son Aaron from premature ageing syndrome, said:

> 'I am a more sensitive person, a more effective pastor, a more sympathetic counsellor because of Aaron's life and death than I would have been without it.'

Am I saying that we need something bad happen to us for us to become a better person, develop a positive outlook or create meaning and purpose for our lives? Absolutely not! Yet a benefit of such life experiences is that it has the propensity to propel us to do more with our lives. Dr Myles Munroe, from his book *Maximizing your Potential*, puts it beautifully:

> 'Circumstances and crises are God's tools to move you into your purpose and the maximizing of your potential.'

One thing is for sure: Life happens! We don't plan for it, but it happens nonetheless. Things come and interrupt our lives. Often, they shake the very core of our foundations; and for some of us, our faith. Questions such as 'why me?' and 'where is God?' rise to the surface. The windstorms of our lives often to leave us with much devastation, pretty much the way a hurricane or tornado does.

If you have experienced this or you are currently facing your own 'windstorm', I want to encourage you with the fact that there is life after such an experience. And how this life pans out is dependent on one thing: You. You get to decide whether to rebuild your life, just the same way Hurricane Katrina survivors had to, or you can choose to sit in the ruins for the rest of your life. The choice is really yours.

However, before you make that choice, let me remind you of two simple facts:

Fact one: Life's traumas or adversity needn't destroy us

As I did more and more research into the subject, I became increasingly convinced of this fact. In an interview, Terry Waite CBE, who was held hostage for 1760 days in Beirut before being released in November 1991, says:

> *'Suffering is always difficult ... But it needn't destroy. Very often it can be turned around so that you can make something creative of it. If you look back into history, you will find that many great acts of creativity came out of suffering.'*
>
> **Source: Open House Program, as heard on Hope 103.2**

With the necessary support, you not only get the opportunity to recover from the experience, but you get the chance to grow as a person. This theory is called Posttraumatic Growth and I will revisit this later. However, the bottom line is, you can experience positive changes and even go on to create a more meaningful and transformed life, in spite of the trauma, challenge or period of adversity you experienced.

Fact two: God can make something positive out of what seems negative

Our world today is proof of this fact. Moreover, we have many examples in the Bible to reassure us. One of my favourite go-to scriptures, in the moments when 'life' happens, is Romans 8:28 that says:

> 'And we know that God causes everything to work together for the good of those who love God and are called according to his purpose for them.'
>
> (NLT)

Whilst we may not be able to see how this could happen from the vantage point of our distressing moments, this fact still holds true. Our responsibility is to keep our hope and trust alive even when we are in the epicentre of our difficult moments.

So how does one make something creative or positive out of one's experiences? How can we be confident that things will work out in the end? What can we do to maintain our hope, peace, and, dare I say, sanity, when it seems our worlds have turned upside down? How can we ensure we keep moving forward and avoid becoming stuck?

Well, *Bounce Back!* has been written with the hope of addressing these questions. As a follow on from *Healing a Discouraged Heart: Getting Back on Track When Life Lets you Down*, *Bounce Back!* aims to share with you different approaches, principles and strategies to help you "bounce back" from whatever life experience you have faced/are facing <u>and</u> support you in creating meaning or purpose for your life.

Whilst you might not be able to see how all this could be, my hope is that by the time you get to the end of this book you will feel enabled to turn your 'test' into a testimony to help others. By that, I don't just mean standing up in church (or any platform) and sharing your testimony, though I believe there is great merit in this. *Bounce Back!*

encourages you to go beyond that. It's about turning your painful experience or 'Your Story' into what I am calling your Pay-it-Forward project, where you proactively take action to help others around you.

The book, *Bounce Back!*, is underpinned by something more powerful. Like Martin Luther King Jnr, I have a dream that one day our world will be filled with more and more people – Christians or not – enabled and mobilised to embark upon their own Individual Social Responsibility (ISR) projects, using a combination of their life experiences (the good, the bad and the ugly), God-given talents and resources, making their 'worlds' a better place. I look forward to that day.

However, before you go off saving the world, let's start with working on 'you' first so that you are positioned to survive, thrive and maximise, taking those lessons from whatever experience you have faced or are facing. If you are ready, let us begin the journey.

How to Use this Book

My intention is to make this book as simple as possible to use. To help you along, I have divided the book into three parts: Surviving, Thriving, and Maximising. By doing so, you can start to see your progress on the journey.

Below are some tips for your journey.

Press pause

I recognise that we have all been on different journeys, which have affected us in different ways. Only you know how yours has affected you. And so I encourage you to take your time as you make your way through this book. Feel free at any point to press 'pause', and continue when you feel ready to do so. It is worth bearing in mind that your journey to personal growth and change will not happen overnight. So find a pace that works for you.

Get the support you need

If you have been through any perturbing or traumatising situation, or have perhaps faced adversity of any sort, it is likely you will need help. Therefore I suggest you get the support you need (e.g. a talking therapy). I leave it to you to decide on the level of support you feel you need. Whatever is the case, there is help out there and you do not need to struggle alone. Furthermore, I have written with the premise that you have or are already receiving help.

Use other available resources

As I have written the following books, I will not necessarily be covering the same ground in depth. So I suggest you consider reading one or more to give you some foundational principles to build on, depending on what you need:

1. *Overcoming Emotional Baggage: A Woman's Guide to Living an Abundant Life*
   (ISBN: 978-0924748738).
2. *Healing a Discouraged Heart: Getting Back on Track When Life Lets you Down*
   (ISBN: 978-0-9562606-3-5).
3. *Quit Hiding, Start Living! How Women Can Free Themselves from Past Hurts*
   (ISBN: 978-0-9562606-6-6).

Reflect and pray

As you make your way through the book, remember to prayerfully reflect on what you have read as well as the questions presented to you. Consider how this applies to you and what changes you feel you can put in place. The changes to aim for are focused around your attitudes, beliefs and behaviours. Once clear on this, be willing to implement what you learn. If you find yourself struggling or resisting with a question or a portion you have read, ask yourself why.

Write your thoughts and ideas down

Use the notes section of this book or any other note-taking device to keep a record of your journey. Things to note down include your thoughts, insights, ideas, and changes you notice. Over time, you can use this to assess your progress. Furthermore, if you are anything like me, you probably get ideas as you read. So rather than jotting them randomly on bits of paper or post-its, capture them in a dedicated place.

Advisory warning!!!

Coach Gladys may show up during the course of this journey. She means you no harm. Her heart's desire is to see you move on. Don't worry: you will get notice when she is about to show up. You then have the option to skip over the page, whistle a tune, or do whatever you fancy. Between you and me, I encourage you to listen to what she has to say, give it some thought, and make your decision afterwards. Remember, she only has your best interests at heart.

The Journey

Why does the journey always seem long?
With windstorms that are often strong.
Time after time, I'm knocked down hard
By life blows with edges of shard.
Bleeding, weeping, I plead with Thee
To take this yoke away from me.

Oh help me God!

You know my desire is to serve You Father
Yet my woes seem to draw me further.
It's not that I don't want do Your will
But doing so feels like struggling uphill.
How I wish I could fly away to rest
To later bounce back and be my best.

Oh help me God!

Now, I'm dosed up with Your love and grace,
At last, I can see myself finishing the race.
It's not that all my storms have gone away,
This time around, I'm determined not to sway,
Pressing on with my purpose, I choose to be fervent
To someday hear, "Well done thy faithful servant."

Oh help me God!

© 2013 Gladys Famoriyo

Introduction

When you hear the words, 'difficult times', 'life challenges', 'pain', 'suffering', and the like, what goes through your mind? Do you wince as you recall memories of hardship or pain? Or perhaps you are in the midst of one such trauma right now?

The reality is that none of us like difficult or hard times. And when they come, rarely (if ever) do we feel adequately prepared for them. Yet, hard times find their way into our lives and we have no choice but to try and deal with them as best we can. And when they arrive, their effects or memories may linger with us for the rest of our days.

One minute you might be fine and at the peak of your game enjoying an awesome career and a loving family, the next, you get test results telling you you have a serious or even life-threatening condition. Maybe you get a call from the school to say your child has gone missing. Or perhaps you were burgled while you were in the house, and now you are a former shadow of your once-bubbly self, refusing to stay at home alone. Maybe you experienced a really bad relationship and suffered at the hands of an abuser. Or perhaps the police showed up at your door to tell you your loved one, who only popped out for five minutes, had been hurt (or even killed) in a road traffic accident. Perhaps you have had to watch a loved one, such as a child or sibling, suffer as a result of terrible illness or addiction that is killing them slowly. Maybe you spent your whole life savings on a business venture, even remortgaging your house, and today, you have lost everything. Perhaps you have experienced the loss of a child, whether in pregnancy, at birth or in infancy. Maybe you have been involved in one of the horrific stories we hear on the news.

Scenarios like these are ones we often don't like to think about and may see as the 'stuff' that happens to other people. Yet bad things happen to good people. I have often been so confounded by this, to the point that it is now on my top 10 list of questions I plan to ask God when I grab a moment of His time in Heaven, when I get there (don't laugh, I am serious).

As for now, I have accepted that life happens. Prior to accepting this, though, I have to admit that I tried another approach: coaxing God to give me advance warning of what's ahead. I did this because in my walk with Him, He often lets me in on His plans for my life. 'So why not this aspect of my life?' I reasoned. That way, I could try to dodge any upcoming potholes. Between you and me, I think we both know what the answer to that was; though I have to say, there were times Father had been gracious enough to at least shout, *'Take the brace position!'* just as they do when an aeroplane is about to crash land.

But my search did not end there.

With today's technology advancing so rapidly, coupled with the comic book and biblical heroes I once read about as a child, the geek in me often wonders why we have not come up with some form of innovative App, or gadget in the form of special high-tech glasses that allow us to see all the bad things ahead – similar to something James Bond might use. That way, we could try stopping bad things from happening. Or perhaps a quick email or text message from God's office, just giving us some more information so we can hang on in there.

Laugh you may, but such quests for answers have been born of my personal frustrations and agonising moments – especially when I've been faced with challenge after challenge with no respite. There have been many times when it felt like I was in an unending and unyielding battle. With no end in sight, you start to grasp for something, anything, to find answers and offer relief. Perhaps you can relate?

Today, I now (fully) accept that life happens and we don't (always) get to know what's about to hit us. The glaring reality is that our journeys can be fraught with 'mountain high' and 'valley low' experiences. Of course, you and I would quite happily skip over all the valley-low times whilst basking in the glitzy and glamorous side of our faith. We would much prefer the testimonies, miracles, breakthroughs, signs and wonders but not the uncomfortable, yet real, side of our faith. However, if you were to consider the bigger picture, you would notice that the times of suffering, hardship and pain are all forerunners of the wonders and signs. Without a test, there cannot be a testimony, nor does a miracle come without a dire situation that calls for one. Just ponder on that for a moment.

Furthermore, central to our faith is the notion of Christ, our Suffering Servant. His suffering culminated with a crucifixion on a cross at Calvary. Yet through His suffering and resurrection we have hope. His torment paved the way for us to have a direct relationship with God. His profound suffering had a positive outcome for us.

So it seems to me that though adversity and trauma find their way into our lives, we too can aim for positive outcomes – for ourselves and others. Moreover, as I began to delve more into God's viewpoint and detach myself from my 'fleshy' responses to life, I realised that I have been sent an advanced memo of what's ahead. It's in John 16:33, and it says:

> *'I have told you these things, so that in Me you may have [perfect] peace and confidence. In the world you have tribulation and trials and distress and frustration; but be of good cheer [take courage; be confident, certain, undaunted]! For I have overcome the world. [I have deprived it of the power to harm you and have conquered it for you.]'*
>
> **(AMP)**

So it seems we were never promised a bed of roses. In trying to manage our expectations with regard to our journey on earth, Jesus informs us that there will be troubling times ahead. He does not sugarcoat this warning. Rather, He tells it like it is. Thankfully, Jesus also builds our hope in His ability to help us overcome, live victoriously, and experience His abiding peace in the storms of life.

With this as the backdrop of this book, my desire is to offer a new perspective when it comes to adversity and life traumas. The ultimate goal is for you and me to bounce back, fortified with hope, grace and strength, whilst using what's in our hands to positively affect change.

Part I – Surviving

Getting to Grips with the Situation

Chapter One

What Doesn't Kill Us ...

You have heard the saying that what doesn't kill us makes us stronger? I have to say I agree with this concept when it comes to adversity and trauma. My take on this is: whilst it is not so much about gaining physical strength (though this may be the case for some), I believe strength comes in many forms. Within the context of the book, it can be seen as growing, maturing, becoming wiser, gaining a new outlook on life, becoming positive, developing compassion for others and embarking a new 'calling'. In short, the outcomes of our challenging life experiences can be positive.

That said, I want to strike a balance here and mention an important point: life hurts and the experience can be distressing for those involved. It would be inhuman to deny this fact. Post-traumatic stress can wreak havoc, and there is an abundance of research to back this up. In spite of this, recent research now suggests that people, over time, can experience growth as a result of this stress.

So, this is the premise I will be looking at in this section.

Flip adversity and trauma on its head

Some years into her happy marriage, Zoe, like a number of women, started to hear her biological clock ticking. Up until that point, she had 'snoozed' the alarm, especially after seeing the horrendous experience a close friend went through with miscarriage and stillbirth. So she threw herself into her successful business. But her biological alarm kept going off. It was then that Zoe realised she had a burning desire to start a family of her own.

Sadly, Zoe's first pregnancy ended in a miscarriage. On that occasion, her way of coping was almost pretending it had never happened, and she got through the pain. Luckily for her, Zoe got pregnant again a couple of months later. But disaster struck again in the form of a missed miscarriage. This time, it was after having her second scan. By now, Zoe felt a bond between her and her baby – stroking her tummy as if to comfort her bundle of joy. But this was not to be, as she was rushed to hospital. A week later, after scans had shown no heartbeat, she delivered her child naturally. Zoe and her husband Andy were devastated – dealing with both the loss of their daughter, who they named Darcy, along with a few people's insensitive comments (including some of the medical staff!). Things were not to improve for Zoe, and two months later she miscarried for the third time.

However, on her fourth attempt, after a 'scary pregnancy', as she put it, Zoe gave birth to a healthy daughter. As you can imagine, she and Andy were overjoyed. They loved being parents and wanted to try again for another child. Thinking the sorrows of miscarriage were behind them, as they had managed a full term pregnancy, they tried again. Both the subsequent pregnancy resulted in a missed miscarriage, meaning she had now miscarried for the fourth time. Zoe and Andy grieved for the loss of each child. To them, they were not just a 'ball of cells', 'potential people' or 'retained products of conception'. They were their precious children, and acknowledged each of them to be so. Zoe said, *'Every child matters, however far in pregnancy a person is'*.

Zoe later went on to have another bundle of joy, a girl, though the journey was not without its perils. Zoe developed a number of health problems. To mar their joy, it was discovered that she was carrying twins, but they lost one of those children, Isabella, who was their fifth and final loss.

Today they have two awesome daughters they dote on. What inspired me about Zoe's story was her strength to pick herself up and keep trying. Time after time she miscarried, but she kept bouncing back and trying again. She said:

'Life may never be normal again when you have been to such depths of darkness, but we can move forward, with as little scar tissue on the soul as possible, and saying goodbye was the key for me."

These powerful words acknowledged the challenges of the journey, the impact it had, and the realisation that moving forward, at times with scars in tow, was the key. This, for me, sums up what our attitude should be towards the traumas and adversity we face.

Zoe's story did not end there. Whilst deciding to move forward, she saw an opportunity to support other people going through a similar journey, to help them say goodbye and move forward. Therefore, Zoe and Andy went on to launch the Mariposa Trust (www.mariposatrust.org), which aims to help people who have been affected by the loss of a child at any stage of pregnancy, at birth or in infancy. The charity offers befriending, support and information. Mariposa is more commonly known under its lead division name, Saying Goodbye (www.sayinggoodbye.org), which offers international remembrance services for people who have lost a child.

Today, Mariposa has extended its reach to the USA (Mariposa International). Furthermore, their website has over 650,000 hits per month, and it supports tens of thousands of people each week – people turning to them when life happened.

Use your life's dramas as a catalyst for positive change

All that Zoe and Andy went on to achieve, after their losses, happened as a result of their tragic experiences with miscarriage. Would they have launched such amazing initiatives had they never had this experience? We will never know. However, through the sad episode of their lives, we see them rise up, enabled with a new strength, to bring hope to many others.

What we see here is what is being referred to as Posttraumatic Growth, a new area in Positive Psychology. Richard Tedeschi and Lawrence Calhoun pioneered this concept through their research. They define posttraumatic growth as:

"*The positive change experienced as a result of the struggle with a major life crisis or a traumatic event.*"

Between the 1980s and 1990s there has been a considerable amount of research studies looking at the positive changes people experience after trauma and adversity, such as victims of rape, war veterans and bereaved adults.

Through their own research, Tedeschi and Calhoun suggest that posttraumatic growth can occur in five general areas:

1. A sense of new opportunities and the opening of new possibilities not previously available.
2. A change in how we relate to others. This can include becoming closer to specific people or developing compassion for others experiencing adversity and trauma.
3. An increased sense of one's own strength: '*If I lived through that, I can face anything*'.
4. A greater appreciation for life in general.

5. A deepening of their spiritual lives and/or change in one's belief system.

Source: www.ptgi.uncc.edu/what-is-ptg

Reflecting back on Zoe and Andy's experience, it is clear that posttraumatic growth had taken place. Perhaps you can relate to one or more of the five growth areas. I know I can certainly tick a number of those boxes myself.

I have to say I am glad that science is now confirming what we already know from the Bible. It's just that now we have a modern term for it. Joseph, Job and the Apostle Paul experienced posttraumatic growth in one or more areas too – each in their own unique way.

With adversity and suffering being inevitable, James 1:2-4 encourages to do the following during trials:

'Dear brothers and sisters, when troubles of any kind come your way, consider it an opportunity for great joy. For you know that when your faith is tested, your endurance has a chance to grow. So let it grow, for when your endurance is fully developed, you will be perfect and complete, needing nothing.'

(NLT)

The New King James Bible suggests we 'Count it all joy ...'. I don't think for a minute the scripture is telling us to act inhuman when life happens. Let's say, for example, you, like Zoe, received the news that your unborn child's heartbeat had stopped. Do you start busting your party moves by disco dancing or do the running man at that news? There would be something wrong with that picture, right?

I don't believe that during difficult times God wants us to override the innate mechanisms He kindly gave us, as humans, to deal with life. These include the ability to grieve over loss, experience pain, and cry. These are normal human responses. If anyone tells you otherwise, just refer him or her to one of the shortest verses in the Bible, i.e. John 11:35, which says, 'Jesus wept' (KJV). He did this after hearing the news of Lazarus's death. This, dear reader, is a typical response to loss/grief, though we all handle it differently.

One thing I have come to value dearly is that what really counts is our steadfast trust in God. I am of the opinion that our reaction to trauma and adversity is often an indicator of what's going on within us. Whilst you might cry, your heart can still remain fully confident in God's power to sustain you and see you through. Yet another person can break down in tears, hopeless and in despair, because they are not anchored in faith. So, though you both cry, you cry for differing reasons and are coming from different places. As the scripture suggests, our situations can then become a litmus test of our proclaimed faith in God. But if we endure in faith, we have the opportunity to grow from that experience, as well as mature in our faith.

Victim or victor? You choose!

A few months ago, I came across a video clip of a young schoolgirl in Guatemala. Her name is Griselda. She was coming back from church in a car with her mother and brother when another car cut in front of theirs. Griselda was dragged out of the car and taken by three men. Those three men raped her.

At thirteen years of age, Griselda now had to live with the trauma of that violation – physically, emotionally, psychologically and spiritually. However, through the work of the International Mission for Justice (IMJ), a Christian global organization that protects the poor from violence in the developing world, Griselda received support through their Aftercare Therapy programme. Furthermore, IMJ supported Griselda in making sure her perpetrators were brought to justice.

The IMJ's trauma therapy was crucial to Griselda's restoration and, through the grace of God, she bounced back. She also found the strength to forgive her perpetrators. But Griselda's story does not end there. In fact, what happened next was nothing short of amazing. Griselda went on to do an internship with IMJ, where she was able to help other girls who had experienced a similar ordeal.

Whilst Griselda never expected to have been raped at the age of thirteen, or at any age for that matter, the sad truth was it happened. However, despite the trauma, it is clear Griselda had experienced posttraumatic growth, in that she developed compassion for others experiencing the same trauma. She also used the opportunity to get involved in something she may not have thought about prior to the incident. In spite of the rape, Griselda decided to make something good come out of her experience. What a testament to God's restorative power her story is. In spite of the ordeal, she has been repositioned to change the lives of others.

There is also another aspect to her growth: her faith. Griselda found the courage and strength in her heart to forgive and move on. For many, this is not the case, and they can remain stuck and/or only see the negative effects of their experiences. In this state, the individual tends to remain a victim of their experience.

What Griselda faced should never have happened. In fact, it should never happen to anyone. But it did. Yet in reading her moving story we see a victor – not a victim. Griselda's story encourages us that there is life and hope after trauma.

Reflective Questions

- Revisit the six growth areas of posttraumatic growth. Which one of these have you experienced, or are currently experiencing?
- Based on how you have handled and/or are handling your challenges, how do you see yourself – victim or victor?
- What do you feel you need to do to help you move forward and grow as a result of your experiences?

Chapter Two

Curb the Spiritual Fits and Holy Tantrums

Ever woke up one day and found yourself having what I call a 'spiritual fit' or a 'holy tantrum'? If you have never experienced this, read on ... perhaps you may discover you actually have.

It's simply one of those days you wake up and, like a child, you start throwing your toys out of the pram. You get into whining and complaining mode. Perhaps you have been holding it 'down', keeping yourself together and trying to cope, but today the walls of your dam broke. You feel abandoned by God and picked on by the devil. On such days, you just want to have a good tantrum. You don't want to pray, read your Bible, go to church, or anything of that nature. Instead, you would rather feed your flesh. I tend to get into eating mode or watching endless, senseless TV.

The day I yelled at God

Some years back, I was going through a particularly trying time. Each new day presented challenges of its own. I kid you not. It was as if a new 'adversity' missile was launched right on cue each morning. It got to the point where I could almost set my watch by it. I tell you, they were relentless. One day, it could be a health challenge, the next, a financial blow. On another day, a relationship issue. Oh, let's not forget the ministry 'dramas' that crop up, which kept me up all night in prayers (and tears). But the one that hit me hard was the major setback regarding one of my purpose-related assignments – something I had invested every resource I had (time, money and effort). Whilst I was still licking my wounds, trying to make head or tail of my circumstances and mustering the strength to get up again, WHAM! Another missile came crashing on me. And the next, and the next …

You know the devil is trying to wreak havoc when even the dependable things in your life no longer become dependable. Within that same period, previously trouble-free household appliances decided to pack up. My good-and-faithful car became terminally ill. Plus, I kept getting non-repairable punctures, and the tyres were <u>not</u> cheap to replace! I was fuming by the time I had to hand over my credit card for the third tyre replacement in a row, within a short period of time.

So you can appreciate my frustration with so many things going wrong at the same time with no breather in between. The financial challenge did not say to the health challenge, *'It's my turn now. So leave Gladys alone now'*. Oh no! They all crowded into my life and occupied every space, moment and ounce of energy. Needless to say, they distracted me no end.

During this time, my mind and spirit became very unsettled. Of course, I knew what the scriptures said about peace, trusting God, and the like, but at that point in time they felt so far removed from me – out of my grasp. Peace became elusive as I tried to deal with my plight. My mind was all over the place. I became distracted and resentful – towards God and others.

Why me? I thought. Didn't God notice what was happening? Why didn't He intervene after all I was serving Him through the ministry and books. Could He not see that all the trials and tribulations were hindering me from doing His work? Why was He allowing this to happen? How could I possibly be in the right frame of mind to minister to other's needs, much less write the books He commissioned, with all this going on in the background?

Arrrrgggghhhh!

Initially I was coping well, maintaining my stance and balance through prayer – trusting in God's awesome ability to turn things around. But that was until I could hold on no more. You know what they say about the final straw that broke the camel's back? Well, that happened to me. I was lying in bed feeling rather rundown, overwhelmed, and stressed out. I was fed up. I had no strength to do anything. I had cried till tears abandoned me. The impetus to get up, read my Bible and pray disappeared. I had no desire to fight, speak in tongues or make any declarations.

I was just sick and tired of the whole situation. I'd just had enough, and I felt the fury brewing within me until the floodgates opened and I found myself boldly shouting at Father:

'CUT ME SOME SLACK!'

In other words, give me a break! Up to that point, I had never done such a thing, as reading the Old Testament as a child kinda made me fear God as One who could zap me away in an instant. But at that moment I did not care about the consequences. In fact, zapping me would have probably done me a favour, I was that fed up. I think I was having my own Elijah moment and just wanted it to end because at least in Heaven we are promised no more pain, sickness, etc.

Me asking Father to 'cut me some slack' was an audacious move on my part, yet I felt it needed to be said. After all, He already knew what was brewing in my heart and if I could not be honest with my Creator, to whom could I bare my soul? As I uttered those words, I was unsure what His response would be. Would I get silence? Would I get a word of encouragement, a vision, or even feel His tangible presence? I did not know what to expect. However, one thing was for sure, I wanted His attention and I needed an answer now.

As I waited patiently in bed, the tears started to stream down my face. I sighed deeply and willed Father to show up in some demonstrable way that I would recognise. I needed Him to rise from His Throne and intervene now. I just wanted to be free from all that was going on. I needed reassurance that He was <u>still</u> standing with me. And you know what, that's exactly what happened. In the silent confines of my bed, I heard Him clearly say, '*I am granting you a reprieve*'.

'Reprieve?' I wondered. Why a reprieve? Plus, I was not sure how the definition of the word related to my situation. Of course, I had a general idea, but I needed to investigate further. So I rolled over in bed, grabbed my phone and opened up my dictionary App. This is something I do frequently when Father speaks to me and I need to understand the words He is using within the context of my situation. I do it in order to get the full gist of what He is saying. And so I started looking up the word. And as I did, it seemed to suggest the cancellation or abandonment of an undesirable event. '*Phew!*' I thought, '*That's a relief!*'

As I pondered, I then realised that Father had answered the brief prayer I'd yelled out in frustration. He had chosen to cancel the pain and suffering the enemy was inflicting on me. I thank God He graciously intervened and said 'peace be still' to all my storms. Immediately, the daily missiles stopped – just like that! For the first time in a long while I was able to BREATHE again, for I had been holding my breath up to that point, bracing myself for the next hit.

When I reflect on that season of my life, I realise that something profound had been taking place. I had always read the scripture that said God would never give us more than we can handle (1 Corinthians 10:13). And in my frustration I was making it clear to Father that

I had reached my limit. And just in case He thought I could handle some more or He had more confidence in my ability to withstand more pain and suffering, I was making it clear that I couldn't. I needed Him to hide me under the shadows of His wings. And, thankfully, He did.

Since that experience I have had more challenges (even worse), but thankfully I have not resorted to yelling my request. Because I had seen Him deliver me in the past, I became confident of His power to save. This is not to say the situations I later faced became less painful or daunting. Rather, some of that frustration has been replaced with trusting Him and learning to enter into His rest (Hebrews 4).

Coach Gee says: Tips for challenging times:
1. Always keep your communication channels open with God in whichever way you can.
2. Find someone who you can confide in and share your concerns. It really does help.

When bad things happen to good people

I remember reading Psalm 73 and breathing a sigh of relief, thinking, *'Thank God I am not the only one'*. Whilst I had read the frustrations of many others, such as Job, Asaph put it so aptly by asking the question, *'Is it in vain*

I have kept my heart pure?'. I love the *Message Bible*, that puts it like this:

> *What's going on here? Is God out to lunch?*
> *Nobody's tending the store.*
> *The wicked get by with everything;*
> *they have it made, piling up riches.*
> *I've been stupid to play by the rules;*
> *what has it gotten me?*
> *A long run of bad luck, that's what—*
> *a slap in the face every time I walk out the door.*
> (Psalm 73:11-14, MSG)

Asaph was asking a poignant question with regard to the purpose of living righteously when it seemed to serve no purpose at all. I suspect many of us today have that question ruminating in our minds. Asaph, like many 'Asaphites' of today, was experiencing hardship to the point where he felt the need to vent his brewing frustrations and inner conflicts.

Today, many 'Asaphs' exist. Some go to church out of duty and some don't. Within both groups are those who have lost their faith. Like the parable of the sower highlights, some of those modern day 'Asaphs' fell away as a result of problems, persecutions, worries and the lure of wealth (Matthew 13). And so, like our dear brother Asaph, they start to weigh up the pros and cons of being a 'goody-two-shoes' when those who haven't been seem to be lapping it up – cruising through life seemingly worry-free.

But had Asaph been incorrect in believing that his right standing with God would safeguard him from the problems he faced? Perhaps he felt short-changed by the fact that bad people seemed to prosper, increased their riches and lived hassle free? Whatever is the case, his frustration was evident in his voice and choice of words.

However, when we read the scripture further, we see Asaph change his stance and answer his own question. He draws some powerful conclusions based on objective observations of his own. He comes to see God as fair and just – rewarding everyone accordingly. He also notices that life is not as rosy for the ungodly either.

Therefore, the secret to not losing 'it' revolves around keeping our gaze heavenward, as opposed to comparing ourselves to others. By the way, those 'others' can include other Christians, especially if they are constantly sharing testimonies when all you have to share are your life dramas.

Furthermore, rather than getting stuck, consider how you can move on from the experience with a view to coming out wiser, stronger, and more mature, with a purpose or goal on which to focus. I think the following quote from Harold Kushner sums up our approach:

'Is there an answer to the question of why bad things happen to good people? ... The response would be ... to forgive the world for not being perfect, to forgive God for not making a better world, to reach out to the people around us, and to go on living despite it all ... no longer asking why something happened, but asking

how we will respond, what we intend to do now that it has happened.'

Apostle Paul puts it beautifully:

'No, dear brothers and sisters, I have not achieved it, but I focus on this one thing: forgetting the past and looking forward to what lies ahead, I press on to reach the end of the race and receive the heavenly prize for which God, through Christ Jesus, is calling us.'

(Philippians 3:13–14, NLT)

The emphasis here is 'forgetting the past', 'looking forward' to the future, 'pressing on', and striving to finish our assignments, depicted here as a race. It is also about focusing on the right things.

Don't throw in the towel

There is a tendency for us to lose our momentum when life happens. There are moments during such times when we seem to lose the drive, focus and strength to carry on. It's akin to trying to do your daily run or gym workout whilst suffering from a bad case of flu. During such times you don't feel like pursuing the dream, goals or God-given assignments you once did with fervour. Furthermore, you may find yourself feeling the same way towards your spiritual activities such as praying, reading your Bible, going to church, and the like.

And so it seems you have taken your hands off the steering wheel.

When I think about losing momentum, I cannot help but think of our dear prophet Elijah. In 1 Kings 18, we observe the prophet accomplish great feats. He challenged the prophets of Baal as a means of demonstrating God's awesome power. He proposed the prophets of Baal built an altar, sacrificed a bull, and called upon their god to bring down fire to engulf the offering. Elijah was going to do the same except that he took the challenge one step further by pouring water on his sacrifice, making it harder for it to ignite. He then called down fire from Heaven to consume the offering. Elijah did this to prove a key point about Gods supernatural ability. Needless to say, he won the challenge and then went on to kill all the prophets of Baal.

I don't know about you, but I felt tired just reading the accounts of everything Elijah did, which included:

- Repairing the altar of the Lord, which had been torn down, using 12 stones.
- Digging a trench around the altar that could take approximately 14 litres of water.
- Piling the wood on the altar.
- Cutting the bull into pieces and laying them on the wood.

It was evident that God was using Elijah mightily. Yet, within a short space of time after his conquest, we see a different side of Elijah. Upon hearing of King Ahab's wife

Jezebel's threat to kill her prophets of Baal, we see Elijah respond in a way that surprised many of us. In 1 Kings 19, Elijah flees to the wilderness and becomes depressed, wanting to die. His words in verse 4 resonate with many of us:

'I have had enough, Lord,'
(NLT)

He came across as fed up after a long bout of 'stuff', which may have included other contributing situations to which we are not made privy. I say this because to see someone switch the way he did may infer there were either other 'things' going on in the background and/or he had experienced persistent challenges. I say this because I can relate. If care is not taken, it can wear you down after a while and make you throw in the towel.

Elijah's story reflects how some of us respond to hardship or challenging times. However, we don't have to throw in the towel in hard times nor do we need to wish to die. Apostle Paul depicted this very well. His middle name could easily be 'hardship' or 'suffering' because that brother faced hell and high water. Yet he kept bouncing back. For that reason, I am awarding him the title, *'Bounce Back Hero'*.

In 2 Corinthians 11:16–33, Paul lists his many 'eye-watering' trials. Other accounts can be found in in:

- 2 Corinthians 1:8–11
- 2 Corinthians 4:8–18

- 1 Thessalonians 2:1–3
- 1 Thessalonians 3:1–8

In reading Apostle Paul's accounts, I sometimes cannot help but wonder what special tonic he was on. Did he eat spinach like Popeye, the cartoon character? OK, joking apart, something must have kept him determined and unyielding when it came to his calling. And even when they tried to keep the brother down in chains whilst in prison he used the opportunity to write his epistles. I can't even begin to imagine what it was like for Apostle Paul in prison. I am pretty sure the conditions weren't great. Yet, despite being in chains, he was focused and motivated, and felt compelled to write the epistles that went on to impact and shape the church we see today. His 'prison' epistles still speak to us today.

And so, whenever I feel I am losing momentum I read the accounts of Apostle Paul to encourage myself. I also draw closer to God to gain strength, courage and the grace to bounce back and press on. Without this, it is likely I would quit what I am supposed to be doing. I also discovered that in such moments, when I cloak myself in God's strength (our proverbial Popeye 'spinach'), I can do what I have been commissioned to do, like continuing to encourage others, even during times of adversity. This is what the scripture in Philippians 4:13 refers to when it says:

> 'For I can do everything through Christ,
> who gives me strength'
> **(NLT)**

This, dear reader, is the crux of this book – pressing on through life, to bring about positive change in our worlds, whilst armed with God's strength and not that of our own. I have come to the conclusion that Apostle Paul was not bionic, nor did he have bones of steel. He felt pain, just like you and I do. Judging by the accounts given in the Bible, he faced situations that would make the rest of us quiver in our boots. But Apostle Paul understood that even whilst battling with thorns in his own flesh, with God's grace he could accomplish all God had for him to do.

Over the years, I have endeavoured to emulate this character trait, i.e. recognising my own human limitations and tapping into Gods strength and grace. Needless to say, two of my books were actually written whilst propped up in bed. Thank God for laptops, tablets, Wi-Fi and mobile technology. Where there is a will there is <u>always</u> a way!

Whilst I am a staunch proponent for resting and taking time out to recover, I realise that there are certain times God may have need for us to accomplish a task on His behalf. But you can be assured that you will receive everything you need with which to do the task, and more.

Coach Gee says:
Whilst the storms of life may rage, our calling never changes, but the mode may have to. Refusing to become adaptable may cost you everything.

Reflective Questions

- Have you had spiritual fits and holy tantrums of your own? If so, what were your symptoms (e.g. not praying, losing faith, etc.)? What situation sparked your response? Looking back, how might you have adapted your attitudes and behaviours?
- Reflecting on your own journey, what can you start to do to help you feel like you are 'forgetting the past', 'looking forward to what lies ahead', 'pressing on', and striving to finish the race – according to Philippians 3: 13–14?

Chapter Three

Handling Life's Unscripted Moments

Each day we wake up to the sad news of one calamity or another, including earthquakes, tsunamis, abductions, mass killings, war, hostage situations, aeroplane disasters, terrorist attacks, murder, and political uprisings. Those who become victims of these situations would never have thought they would find themselves embroiled in such horrors. Yet they have to face the sad reality of their situation.

Whilst you may not find yourself in any of these predicaments, you will certainly experience unscripted moments of your own. There will be a day when calamity strikes. Paraphrasing Job's sentiments in Job 3:25:

*'The thing I greatly feared has come upon me,
And what I dreaded has happened to me.'*
(NLT)

That phone call, letter or news that knocks you for six. The negative outcome you were hoping to avoid now stares you in the face. The tragedy, the pain, the shame, the disappointment, the hurt, the abuse ... and the list goes on.

So what do you do?

When calamity strikes, press on

It is interesting how, for some of us, just the day before calamity struck, we were lifting up holy hands in church, declaring the greatness of God. You sang, you cried, you danced! You felt the presence of God right there, and you were reassured of His love for you. The word the preacher preached was on point, and you joined the choruses of 'amen' and 'hallelujah', agreeing to that fact. You met up with a friend in the church foyer, one who was going through a rough time, and reminded them that God is faithful and He will come through.

However, in the blinking of an eye, all that seems to have faded away into the background. For today, the very thing you have dreaded has happened. It has rocked the very foundation of your world and is now gnawing away at your faith. Your world, as you know it, seems to be falling apart. And may never be the same. Your hope and strength seems to ebb away by the second as you try to make sense of what's going on.

This is what I refer to as one of life's *unscripted moments* – situations we simply find ourselves in. So what do we do? Do we abandon ship or run for the hills? The reality is, we must face whatever it is and tackle it as best we can. This is certainly not a time to bury your head in the sand or even pretend that everything is OK. Doing so can have great repercussions of the negative kind.

There is one woman I truly admire when it comes to handling an unscripted moment, and that was the woman with the issue of blood. Luke 8:40–48 tells us of a nameless woman who had had a bleeding disorder. We don't know much about her except the fact that she had been suffering for twelve years. In seeking a solution for her malady, she had suffered at the hands of many so-called healers. And despite all her efforts, her bleeding persisted.

This woman must have suffered on many levels, as a result of her condition:

- **Physically:** She would have become anaemic, meaning she would have experienced fatigue, breathlessness, lethargy, faintness and headache. She may have had a pale complexion, dry/flaking/spoon-shaped nails, and painful ulcers at the corners of her mouth. I suspect this condition may have also aged her, making her look older than she actually was.
- **Financially:** Some manuscripts say she had spent everything she had on doctors. So perhaps she initially had some money, but later ended up draining all her resources till there was nothing left. So even if the most celebrated guru or consultant of her day had showed up in town, she would have had nothing left to give.

- **Socially**: This woman would have been classed as ceremoniously unclean owing to her discharge. This meant she wouldn't have been able to sit in a gathering, such as church, at the risk of contaminating others. I'm wondering whether she was separated from loved ones, or even abandoned. Ostracised from her community, she must have felt isolated, and would have had to struggle on her own.

Take a moment to consider this: imagine every waking moment of your life is affected by such a condition. You would have to think twice, and plan for even the most basic of things, such as fetching water at the local well or buying food in the marketplace.

Despite this going on in the background, we read about her mustering the little energy she had, coupled with her faith, to seek out this new Healer she had heard was in town. You and I would both agree that she would have been justified should she had chosen to stay in bed that day. Yet she chose to get up because she had the deep conviction and hope that she would be healed. She believed if she could just touch Jesus' garment, she would be healed of her suffering. And that is what happened. Her faith and determination paid off, and was even commended by Jesus. In touching Him, she was made whole.

Though this lady is nameless, she continues to inspire us as an example of how to handle an unscripted moment. She had every reason to give up because the situation looked hopeless and dire. Plus, she had tried and tried so many times, seeing so many so-called physicians who had failed her. She could have given up any hope of ever being restored to health. But she didn't. I suspect she was driven by a hope of a better future.

Reflecting on this determined woman's plight, we have to remember that there was no National Health Service (NHS) nor were there any of the treatments or medication we have readily available today. There is no mention of any family, friend or advocate to stand by her. It is likely she had never expected the previous twelve years to pan out the way they did. But it happened. However, in spite of all of that, her incredible story of relentless pursuit inspires us. This woman pressed on regardless, even when life hurt. She also deserves a *'Bounce Back Hero'* award.

There is so much to learn from this lady and I hope and pray that as you reflect on your own situation you are encouraged to keep pressing on when 'life' happens.

Keep digging for gold

In my quest to find answers as to why some people fare better than others in the face of adversity, trauma or challenging times, I always marvel and become inspired at the lengths some will go to overcome what they were facing. One such story was that of Dela Idowu and her plight to find a kidney for her brother.

In 2011, her brother Tayo was diagnosed with end-stage kidney failure. As his only sibling, she offered to be his living kidney donor so that he could have a life-saving kidney transplant. However, nothing could have prepared her for the journey ahead. Though it was an exciting time with the prospect of helping her ailing brother, Dela went through a rollercoaster of emotions. Sadly, after months of medical tests, doctors told her that she couldn't donate her kidney as her own health might be put at risk should she do so.

As you can imagine, Dela was devastated at the news, as she desperately wanted to help her brother. She said, '*I wallowed alone in my grief as I knew Tayo could wait years for a transplant because of the lack of organ donors from the African Caribbean community*'.

However, after several months Dela decided she was going to use her experience as a potential living donor to effect a positive change in her community and raise awareness of the benefits of being an organ donor. In doing so, she was convinced that countless lives could potentially be changed and transformed. Dela wanted her story to inspire others to come forward as a donor for a loved one with kidney failure. And so she embarked her incredible journey.

Dela went on to set up 'Gift of Living Donation' (G.O.L.D.), a community interest company, to improve kidney donation and transplantation within the black community. She approached the NHS to fund a short film on living kidney donation, aimed to raise awareness within the black community. Sadly, Dela was turned down, but that did not deter her. The rejection made her more determined than ever to raise the necessary capital to produce *We Are Family* independently, a short film on living donation, which targets the black community.

To her credit and as a result of her dedication to the cause, Dela went on to produce what is now considered to be one of the best resources on living kidney donation for the black and minority ethnic (BME) community in the UK. She teamed up with nurse specialists in various hospitals across the UK, who saw the film as a valuable resource to help raise awareness of the plight of kidney patients of African Caribbean heritage waiting for a transplant. The short film aims to help people start having the difficult conversation of organ donation with their families.

As a result of Dela's film, an increasing number of family members have been coming forward as donors. In doing so, their beautiful gift of organ donation has helped their loved ones regain their health and, ultimately, their lives.

For Dela, greater news was to come. On October 15th, 2014, her brother Tayo finally received his life-saving transplant after waiting for five years. Seeing the transformation in his life and knowing that he had a brighter future ahead was fantastic to see. It was worth the years of effort. Dela said,

'It has been an amazing journey which has come full circle. It was challenging, with many ups and downs and obstacles, but with passion, drive and having a 'never give up' spirit, ordinary people just like me can do extraordinary things that can change a person's life.'

In addition to the short film she wrote and produced, Dela also wrote a book, titled *More than a Match: One Family's Uplifting Experience of Living Kidney Donation.*

Dela's moving story goes to prove that if you keep digging, one day you will strike gold. It is interesting to see how she refused to give up after being told she couldn't be a living donor herself or when she was turned down for funding to produce the movie. At both points, Dela could have given up, thinking to herself, *'Oh well, at least I tried'*. But oh no! She was not taking 'no' for an answer as her brother's life was at stake, along with many others from the BME community. So she persisted, and many lives have been saved and/or improved as a result of her tenacity to keep 'digging'.

Perhaps you have had knock-backs of your own on your mission to turn a bad situation around. Each time you rise up, it seems everything and everyone is intent on knocking you down again. If that is where you are, my hope and prayer for you is that as you continue to read this book you become unstoppable in your quest. I pray you receive all you need to do what your heart keeps nudging you to do. So stand in faith, be encouraged, and keep searching for your goldmine. It is out there.

Avoid the blame game

When I misplace something, like a set of keys, or my plans have gone awry, my first approach is to start searching for answers. For example, if I were to lose a set of keys I would start by trying to retrace my steps. If a plan does not work out, I go back to the drawing board and consider what went wrong. By doing this I hope to get to the root cause; and, if I'm honest, find something or someone to blame.

When calamity strikes I find myself adopting the same approach, as I suspect you do too. We start searching under every nook and cranny, trying to uncover spiritual answers to our earthly problems. And we can end up spending a lifetime searching for answers and never finding one. However, the answer to our earthly challenges is rarely straightforward, as there could be many contributory factors.

One such is the fact that we have been embroiled in spiritual battles daily, as a result of carrying our cross and surrendering our lives to Christ. This has meant that there have been trials and tribulations assigned to us. Ephesians 6:10–12 encourages us with the following:

> 'A final word: Be strong in the Lord and in his mighty power. Put on all of God's armor so that you will be able to stand firm against all strategies of the devil. For we are not fighting against flesh-and-blood enemies, but against evil rulers and authorities of the unseen world, against mighty powers in this dark world, and against evil spirits in the heavenly places."
> (NLT)

Whether we like it or not, we are in a war, fighting our unseen opponents. And we stand firm against them through prayers and the other spiritual weaponry available to us, though attacks still come (see Ephesians 6:13–20). Furthermore, there is always that chance that we have become embroiled in a heavenly wager, as we saw in the life of Job, who chose to live righteously.

I have found that we are sometimes quick to blame ourselves (or others) for sinning or not praying/studying/fasting enough, not having enough faith, and the like. If this is where you are at, I would like you to press pause for a moment. Whilst all these have consequences and can cause problems in our lives, I suggest you consider the following.

The battle is not always ours to fight

Whilst there were times God asked His children in the Bible to fight against the enemy, there were also times He told others, like Jehoshaphat, to *'stand still and see the salvation of the Lord'* when he faced war (2 Chronicles 20). So, sometimes, I believe it is not so much about how much activity we carry out, praying louder, longer, harder (though prayer is necessary), as about seeking God for the correct strategy for each situation presented to us. In doing so, we are affirming our faith in His ability to deliver us.

I have known times when it was clear that Father was calling me to rise up and fight. And there were others when I was told to be still. So perhaps now is a good time to tune in to see what God might be telling you. There is no point in getting emotional or doing what you have always done, because that strategy may not work for this particular battle you are facing.

By the way, let me add here that all the spiritual activities I mentioned before are a must for our development as Christians. However, I feel there is a problem when we feel our formulaic approaches will always yield us what we want. As you and I know, this is not always the case. Plus, we don't leave room for God to be God and allow His perfect will to be done. By following a set formula, we run the risk of succumbing to the notion of self-sufficiency, which cannot co-exist with our complete reliance on God. Plus, trying to do it ourselves often means we get it wrong. I feel we need to be walking in sync more with God.

Whilst standing still in faith may seem strange to you, especially as you have a major battle in full swing, you may want to adopt this stance, especially if you don't know what to do. I have found strength and direction in the quiet, still moments – the times when I block out the noise of the battle. I have experienced phenomenal breakthroughs and victories when I have sat still and prayed silently. So my point is, tune in to God and see what He would have you do.

It is not always about sin

This tends to be one of the top three reasons we use to rationalise what's going on in our lives. As mentioned before, there is a consequence to our actions – both the good, the bad and the ugly. Sin can open doors to all manner of issues and it could be quite easy to jump to the conclusion that it is the root cause. But in such a frantic state, there is a high chance we misdiagnose or misread the situation either by pointing the finger at ourselves, or at others (e.g. family members – living or dead). In fact, others may have told you that this was the case. So what next?

Well, whilst I am all for confessing sin and repenting, as the Bible tells us to (trust me, you don't want to remain in this state), I am also comforted to know that we all sin and fall short every day! And because of that, God made provision for a Sacrificial Lamb to die on the cross for our sins (Romans 3:23). We sinners are declared to be in right standing with God when we believe in Jesus. The precious blood of Jesus still works on our behalf today, though this is no license to sin. It's because of God's grace that we are not consumed. It's because of this grace that rain falls and the sun shines on both those who serve God and on those who don't.

So before you blame yourself for something you did or did not do, I recommend you ask the Holy Spirit, the Spirit of Truth, to reveal what is going on.

By the way, I hope you realise that the absence of adversity or challenging life moments is not an indication of an absence of a sinful life! So I want to make it clear that every predicament in our lives has not necessarily come about as a result of sin, though some may want to argue that suffering originated from the sin in the Garden of Eden. Whilst I will not be using this book to get into such biblical arguments, which, frankly, won't help you right now, one thing is clear from the Bible – many suffered for their faith. And if this happened to them, it can happen to us too.

Coach Gee says:
Though the accuser of the brethren (i.e. the devil) is always throwing accusations, don't give him fodder to feed on. Prayerfully do some soul searching regularly (i.e. not just when trouble comes up) to become more self-aware, and so you can take action when necessary.

Reflective Questions

- Referring back to the story of the woman with the issue of bloods, take a moment to consider how you are or have handled unscripted moments of your own. What were your attitude and behaviours like? What might you do differently?
- Has God given you a strategy for this season? Perhaps now is a good time to tune in to see what God might be telling you.
- Now is a good time to examine your heart. Are you still standing in faith? Have you drifted away from God? Do you need to up your game concerning your quiet times e.g. praying, studying of the Word, etc.? Only you can answer these questions.

Part II – Thriving

Rebuilding your Foundations

Chapter Four

Maximise your Downtime

One of the blessings of having some downtime is being able to take your foot off the throttle and have some 'me' time. This time affords you the luxury of the five Rs: rest, recover, replenish, reflect, and regroup. For anyone going through a tough time, I strongly recommend this so as to ensure you come back stronger, better and wiser.

Embrace your seasons

Some years ago, I was talking to a friend about how I was feeling. She shared with me a simple principle: accept that life has happened and acknowledge it by taking the necessary actions.

The fact was, I had never given myself the permission to do this. My response to life's challenges was always to forge ahead at full speed – the opposite to some. Whilst you may think this is a good approach, especially seeing this book is about moving forward, there has to be time set aside to slow down or pause to take stock of the situation. More importantly, time is required to make the necessary adjustments or take the action that the situation necessitates.

Instead, what I was doing was brushing the situation off and pushing myself to keep forging ahead – at times without having the necessary respite or support to help me overcome the challenges I faced. This meant I was stockpiling a barrage of spiritual, physical and emotional issues, precariously, without dealing with them or managing their effect on me. I was erroneous in believing that as long as I carried on, all the while applying sprinklings of my spiritual activities, such as praying, reading of the Bible and attending church, that this would do.

All life situations are not equal

A trap I fell into was treating all my challenges the same way, instead of aligning my response to each situation I faced. To illustrate this point, consider this:

If you have a headache, your default response might be to take a painkiller like Paracetamol. When I have a headache, I have discovered it is my body's way of telling me that I am either in need of food or sleep. And so to deal with my headache, it is likely that I'll take a nap, eat, take a painkiller, or do all of the above.

However, a different cause of action is needed if you suspect you are having a heart attack or stroke. Due to the severity of the condition, you will need to be taken to hospital where you can get urgent medical attention. Treat either of those as if you have a headache, and you may find yourself in a serious, possibly life-threatening, situation.

Therefore, the onus is on us to correctly decipher what we are facing and get the necessary support to overcome the problem. It is wrong to think that all life challenges are the same. We cannot simply paint them all with the same brush and hope for the best. Yet this is how we sometimes treat our perturbing situations.

Treat your situations accordingly

I remember after having surgery, some years back, to remove a bunion on my foot, I was told I would need to stay off my feet for up to eight weeks. I was treated as a day patient and was sent home after the surgery because it had not required a general anaesthetic. Indeed I was conscious and managed to see the whole thing (don't tell the surgeon, but his surgical glasses were completely reflective and I was thrilled to see what was going on). Because a general anaesthetic had not been administered there was no need to keep me in. So they sent me on my merry way with instructions on what I needed to do before my first follow-up appointment. This included exercising the toe (yikes ... now that was painful), being off work, and generally taking things easy. These instructions were given so I could recover from the surgery and fully regain the use of my foot.

However, there was another time I needed to have my four wisdom teeth taken out. On this occasion, I was admitted into hospital and given a general anaesthetic. It was just as well, as the pain would have been too much for me to bear, unlike that of a regular tooth extraction. Moreover, to complicate matters, all four teeth were impacted, so a lot of work was required.

After the extraction, I was kept in hospital overnight – partly because the surgery took place late in the day and I was still groggy as a result of the anaesthetic. By the following day, I was well enough to go home and was given instructions as to what I could and could not eat while I was on the mend. The recuperation for this operation turned out to be a lot quicker than that for the bunion. It also meant I lost weight as I was on a liquid diet initially. With the bunion operation I needed to rest my foot for six to eight weeks, doing very little movement, meaning I gained some weight (☹).

I know I have gone to some length to describe these two surgeries, but I wanted to highlight how they each required different courses of treatment and recovery strategies. Can you imagine if I had tried to resume eating and chewing immediately after the teeth extraction or if I had attempted to wear a shoe immediately after the bunion surgery? It is likely I would have done myself some damage, as well as delaying my recovery.

Well, the same applies to your life experiences. There is a chance you could be doing damage to yourself or delaying your recovery when you fail to embrace what's currently going on in your world. So now is a good time to face the facts.

Stop fighting change!

Recently, I had an interesting conversation with a lady who made me smile as she told me her story. My smile was not because I was making light of her situation. Rather, it was because she reminded me of someone – a version of myself, many years ago.

She was telling me of a recent health challenge she had suffered; and being an 'A' type personality, her response to the situation did not surprise me at all. Despite being ill, she did not see why her busy schedule had to stop – even for a very serious health condition. After all, she had a busy career and children that 'needed' her.

She told me of the time she collapsed and was about to be rushed to hospital. Her response? 'I don't have the time to go to hospital!' After she was persuaded to go, she became very impatient with the hospital staff when they could not give her an immediate diagnosis. Then, when the doctors ran test after test and could not give her an answer, she fumed at what she presumed to be their incompetence. You can imagine her annoyance when she was told they needed to keep her in for a few days to run more tests. She was livid! Her response was, *'I don't have the time for this'*. The doctors tried to explain that her collapse gave them cause for concern, and that her condition needed to be investigated.

You see, patience was not her thing. Nor was sitting around and doing nothing, because, according to her, she had lots to do. As far as she was concerned, she was wasting time being in hospital. Moreover, she felt she was no longer in control of her world. She was used to taking charge and working on her own terms. Now it seemed this had been taken away from her. Being forced to take what I fondly call 'enforced rest' did not appeal to her, and as you can imagine, the notion of relaxing or not stressing was foreign to her. Her lifestyle up till then involved constantly being on the go – on full throttle.

One thing she kept telling me was she had no time for illness. On the surface, this could be seen as a good stance to adopt, driven by your passions and purpose. They do say, 'You can't keep a good man down' as they often bounce back from setbacks. However, a wise man also recognises that there are some situations that even they cannot control, such as those that concern their health. So the right approach would be to maximise their downtime by getting better, whilst keeping in mind that their being 'down' does not necessarily mean they are 'out'. One can still be productive, even in this season, though it is most likely going to need a different approach. I will discuss this later.

As I continued to listen to this lady, it became clear she had an issue with relinquishing control. It was also clear to me that Father was orchestrating a healing experience in her body, along with her soul and spirit, though she was resisting this vehemently. I could see that the healing process was going to extend beyond her physical needs. Part of this 'downtime' was meant to create an opportunity to enrich her relationship with God. This is something myself and others have experienced. It is amazing that though the physical body may be 'down', rendering us immobile and/or inactive, it becomes an opportunity for the human spirit and soul to be revived and restored, and to experience growth. So much good can come out of such times. Therefore fighting it is not the solution.

Another challenge we sometimes have with letting go is that we can get completely obsessed with the notion that the world could not possibly function without us. This sets us up for so many traps, including self-sufficiency and pride. I can relate to this, and, looking back, I can see that whenever I failed to relinquish control it was akin to me telling God, *'Father, don't worry, I've got this covered. You just sit on Your throne'.* And while I fight for control I give God no room for Him to be God. It becomes a power struggle, though Father will sit and watch you try to conquer the world yourself ... that is, until you come back to your senses.

I have noted that when we refuse to let go, it can be an indicator of trust issues underpinning our behaviours. As I write, the scripture in Hebrews 4 comes to mind where is says the people did not enter God's rest because they did not mix faith with the Word. In doing this too, we struggle in our own strength and never get to enjoy simply resting in God's capable arms. And so we spend huge chunks of our lives resisting the great things God has in store for us.

In closing, I want to let you know that relinquishing control is not a sign of weakness nor does it mean you have given up. On the contrary. It is a great sign of strength, courage, hope and faith. And what you are doing is setting yourself up for an even greater season of your life. Trust me, after what you have been through you NEED Him to help you bounce back to accomplish great things. So, why not let God be God?

Don't let your 'issues' rob you of your potential to be great

One of my passions in life is to help people identify their 'issues' so they can get the help they need, freeing them to pursue their God-given purpose. This continues to be the underlying intention of all my books, including *Overcoming Emotional Baggage*, *Healing a Discouraged Heart* and *Quit Hiding, Start Living!*.

I hold the view that whilst knowledge is power, self-awareness is a much needed skill to aid us in making smarter choices and better decisions for our lives. Without this, we stand the risk of accumulating a number of unresolved issues and even emotional baggage as we make our way through life's twists and turns. In turn, these can affect us in a number of ways e.g. spiritually, socially, physically, mentally and behaviourally. Furthermore, seeing as our attitudes and behaviours underpin our actions, there is a great need to ensure our actions are not issue/baggage-driven.

In the following section, I will show you how our issues can affect us through the lives of two women.

'Enough is enough!'

Some years ago I met an elderly lady who I will refer to as Doris. She had been married to her husband for close on 40 years. And all through those years, he had physically and emotionally abused her. Shortly before I met Doris, her husband had become very ill, unable to take care of himself, and he was in need of fulltime care. Doris assumed this role and confided in me that, despite the 24/7 care she gave him, he was continuing to abuse her.

When I took a peek behind the curtains of Doris' life, the story of a young girl who had grown up with abuse unfolded. Not just suffering at the hands of her father, who was physically and emotionally abusive, but her boyfriends too, starting at the tender age of fifteen. So it would seem that everyone she loved and who claimed to love her too abused her in one way or another, including her husband of 40 years. Living with the shame and a barrage of negative emotions, Doris did not feel she could tell anyone – that was until she opened up to me. And she did this because she had finally become fed up of a lifetime of abuse.

Coach Gee says:
Whilst the subject of domestic violence (or any abuse) goes beyond the focus of this book, I would encourage anyone going through this to <u>please</u> get some help.

Mother, behold your daughter

Recently, a young lady, who I will refer to as Kim, approached me and shared her story with tears streaming down her face. She had been waiting to have a child for some years. So you can imagine the joy she experienced when she finally conceived. Kim went on to have a bouncing baby girl and was over the moon. However, her little girl was diagnosed as having an autistic spectrum disorder. This news rocked the foundation of Kim's world. She became extremely angry with God for *'doing this to her'*, as she put it, especially after having to wait such a long time to have a child.

Shortly after her daughter's diagnosis, Kim told me she found herself resenting her daughter, and was struggling to build the mother-child bond. As the child was growing up, this became increasingly noticeable, and on most occasions it was her husband who tended to their daughter's needs. It was as if Kim could not reconcile herself to the fact that she now had an autistic child that had special needs. Somewhere deep inside, Kim couldn't make a connection with her daughter. At the time I met Kim, their daughter was eight years old.

Again, when I asked about her past, Kim told me she had grown up in an environment where she experienced both emotional neglect and emotional abuse from her guardians. The abuse intensified whenever Kim did anything wrong, including not being the best in any activity or excelling at school. She recalls anything 'bad' in her guardian's eyes resulted in a combination of little or no affection and attention except for the name-calling and badgering. When I asked about her relationship with her husband, she confessed, after a period of silence, that her marriage was not great. She went on to tell me she was struggling to make it work and felt her own unresolved childhood issues had a lot to do with the problems. Now, it seemed, both her marriage and child were suffering because of these issues.

* * *

I can go on with story after story of people I have come across who were struggling with their unresolved issues and emotional baggage – some which occurred in their formative years, as was the case with Doris and Kim. We see the impact of these issues years later, when they go on to affect their relationships (with partners, children and God) and their own personal growth.

This also meant they were stuck as a result of their life-challenging moments. In such a state, it is difficult to press on with our journey, much less our purpose. For example, Kim's potential and purpose, that of being a great mother, is jeopardised whilst she turns her back on her child. And their beautiful daughter gets robbed of the opportunity to be raised by a godly mother. And then, just like many children who suffer rejection from a parent, guardian or anyone they look up to, often, they end up accumulating issues of their own. And so the cycle continues.

So the onus is on you, as an individual, to deal with your unresolved issues along with the negative emotions that have risen as a result of your difficult situations, because they will <u>always</u> hold you back. In fact, I would say there's no point ploughing through the rest of the book if you choose to do otherwise, because like untreated weeds, they will continue to show up. Your future and purpose here on earth may be jeopardised (sounds dramatic but it is true). You will struggle to make the most of your God-given talents and potential. You will never be the best you can be, and at best we only get to see a pale copy of the real you ... with the real you taking a back seat. This, dear reader, is what I refer to as the *'female hybrid syndrome'* in my book, Overcoming Emotional Baggage. This is really no place for anyone.

Perhaps you have come to recognise unresolved issues of your own? Or maybe you are struggling with negative emotions such as lack of forgiveness towards those who have treated you badly, or towards God, whom you felt could have stopped it. There may be a part of you that wants to see justice done or get your wrongdoers to say 'sorry' but the reality is that this may never happen. They say that holding on to resentment and being unwilling to forgive is like drinking poison and hoping it will harm your perpetrator. It is you it harms. Furthermore, you, my dear reader, remain the prisoner whilst you choose to live this way. And yes ... it is a choice.

Coach Gee says:
Choose today to take the first step to an issue-free, baggage-free life. Get the support you need to overcome this, freeing

yourself from entanglements that will most certainly hold you back. Above all, bring the situation to God and ask Him to completely heal and restore you.

Reflective Questions

- How can you apply the 5Rs to your life right now: rest, recover, replenish, reflect, and regroup?
- Have you accepted the situation you are facing or have faced in the past? Do you have a clear understanding of how it has affected you? Are your current attitudes and behaviours adequate in helping you bounce back? If not, consider changing your approach.
- Are there areas of your life you are resisting or refusing to relinquish control of? If so, ask yourself why? What's driving that? If you were to take one action today to help you feel like you are no longer resisting change, what would that be?
- Is there a chance you may have any unresolved issues or negative emotions? How are these showing up today? What impact is it having on various areas of your life such as your relationships, behaviours, wellbeing, job/career, etc.? What do you feel needs to happen to help you overcome these? PS: You may find reading *Overcoming Emotional Baggage: A Woman's Guide to Living an Abundant Life* useful.

Chapter Five

Get Back in the Saddle

This chapter is all about taking steps towards working on you, as a person, with the goal of getting you on top form. It is also about equipping you so you are ready for whatever happens next in your life.

Change your perspectives

How do you view life? Is the cup typically half full or half empty? You may think you see the cup half full, but is this the case all the time? Ponder your situation right now? What's your outlook on it? Do you see a dead-end there or do you see an opportunity for God to perform a miracle? Is it all doom and gloom or is there a silver lining under the dark cloud?

Everything you do in life and every step you take (or don't take) hinges on your underlying beliefs and attitudes. I love Henry Ford's quote:

> *'If you think you can do a thing or think you can't do a thing, you're right.'*

However, Henry was not the first to highlight this point. The Bible also makes the point in the book of Proverbs 23:7:

> *'For as he thinks in his heart, so is he.'*
> **(NKJ)**

So it is worth reflecting on the contents of your heart because the sad reality is that they can end up betraying you. You might profess in church or anywhere else that you trust God, all the while, deep down, you are wracked with fear and anxiety in the face of your trial. Perhaps you did not start off that way and you have tried to hold on as hard as you can, but today you are struggling to see how this hopeless situation can be turned around. Let me share a story with you.

Choose to see the cup half full

I recently heard a testimony of a young bride who was looking forward to becoming a mother. After her first child, she found a lump in her breast. Sadly, the lump was diagnosed as malignant and she had to go through aggressive chemotherapy. She was also told that it was unlikely she would have any more children. However, this lady, who I will refer to as Jane, prayed. She was led to a particular scripture in John 11:4 that says:

> '*This sickness is not unto death, but for the glory of God, that the Son of God may be glorified through it.*'
>
> (NKJV)

These were the words Jesus proclaimed when Mary and Martha sent a message to Him about Lazarus's sickness. She held on to the scripture in faith. Thankfully, the cancer treatment worked and, not only that, she went on to have more children. Years later, the cancer came back and she had to go through another round of chemotherapy. Whilst the treatment worked, unfortunately the aggressive nature of the treatment brought about chemo-induced heart failure, something she was told would substantially diminish her quality of life.

Yet, despite this negative prognosis, Jane stood on the promised Word and had the support of many standing with her. As she shared her trials of the last twenty years, I could not help but marvel at her courage and determination. And I doubt there were many dry eyes in the audience as we were all encouraged and inspired by her wonderful testimony. Today, she is the picture of complete health!

When I hear of such courage in the face of many trials, I am reminded of the faithfulness of God through our lives. But there are two sides of the story. Indeed, God is faithful but He also requires our complete trust. Our hope and trust in God fashions our outlook. If you don't think He is able to help you overcome your situation or give you the grace to walk the journey then you may well stay in that same 'stuck' place. And, I would venture to say, your cup is half empty.

Remember the story of Kim I mentioned earlier? To her, the situation with her autistic daughter was hopeless. Plus, her sentiment was *'this was not the kind of life I signed up for when I got married'*. Kim's 'half-empty' cup is one attitude. Yet, there is another.

I met a lady a while back whose first-born was diagnosed as having special needs. I will call her Mary. Mary's reaction to this news was a complete contrast to Kim's. Being faced with the fact that this special addition to their family would mean a complete change to their previous ideas of parenting, she cracked on. Her stance was, *'Well, let's get on with it!'* Rolling up her sleeves, she and her husband threw themselves into raising their wonderful son. She read all she could find about his condition, found out what support was available, and was determined in her heart to be the best parent she could be to their son. Mary went on to have more children and, if anything, her experience with her son taught her to cherish and treat each child as a unique individual. No doubt Mary faced bumps in the road but her stance was the same. She took the 'half-full' cup attitude and was the better for it. To me, Mary deserves one of our Bounce Back Hero awards.

Align your perspectives with God's Words

How often do you say, *'Well, let's get on with it!'* when facing a challenge? By the way, I do recognise that we all have differing stories and life experiences. Owing to other factors, such as our personalities, our previous experiences, and our upbringing, they all contribute to how we respond. For example, some of us may take a bit longer than others to accept the situation and do something about it, whereas others embrace it and crack on.

That said, regardless of our individual 'make-up', ultimately we have a common union in God through Christ. Regardless of what we have faced, we can all converge on biblical truths that Father has made available for us, to be applied when needed. This bolsters us and gives us strength when we have none of our own. Trying to get on with things, relying solely on our own strength is futile! The fact is life happens and life hurts! Hence, as we all have equal access to the Word – you, just as much as the next person – our challenge becomes whether we believe and digest its content so it can bear fruit whilst anchoring our souls.

I do believe that keeping His Word in our heart will give us what we need in tough times. So it helps to plant the seeds of the Word in your heart – both in season and out. Then when there is a need for it, the fountain of God's life-giving Word springs forth from the inside. I remember times of personal crisis when I did not have access to a physical Bible or my Bible App on my phone. Yet what I had planted in my heart, many years ago, sprang to life and reminded me of God's Word.

So, if you feel your perspective needs to be aligned with God's, take a dive into His Word. If you feel like you are facing a hopeless situation, take your pick of a number of stories where God achieved the impossible. When I am in doubt, I recollect how God gave Abraham and Sarah a son at the age of 100 and 90 years respectively (Genesis 15–21). If facing a 'Goliath' of a situation, I remind myself of David's victory against the giant (1 Samuel 17). When I cannot see a way out of any situation, I read how God delivered Jehoshaphat miraculously without him having to fight his way out of a war (2 Chronicles 20). That's the God we serve.

Coach Gee says:
Pay attention to what you watch and listen to as they can influence your perspective more than you realise.

Adapt to your seasons

I'm always inspired when I watch on TV the story of someone who is relearning how to walk as a result of the loss of one or more limbs or through illness. As you can imagine, this tends to be a long, painful and hard journey. Their journeys are filled with high points like the very first time they take a step unaided or when they manage to walk a particular distance. What a joyous occasion that is. And then there are the times they face setbacks, when it feels like one step forward and two steps back. No doubt there are times when they feel disheartened at their progress. Yet they keep at it because they realise that each day they take steps towards becoming independently mobile again.

These individuals are a classic example of people adapting to their seasons. They are choosing not to give up, despite the adversity or trauma they must have faced that required them to relearn how to walk. This may seem like a huge mountain to climb, but with determination, the right attitude, the right therapy programme along with a network of support in the form of therapists, doctors, family, friends and well-wishers, walking can become a reality for them over a period of time.

It takes guts to look at your present situation, as bad as it may seem, yet decide this 'thing' is not going to keep you down. It takes strength of character to say, *'you know what? I'm going to forge ahead'* even though you know the journey will be hard. It takes a certain mindset to embrace change and be willing to take the necessary action to get to your destination.

The reality for some of us is that we get stuck somewhere between adjusting our minds and taking the relevant action. If you are resisting the change, your mind has not adjusted and it is unlikely you will reach your goal even if you have a whole team of people supporting you. In fact, you may end up being disruptive. Your challenge now is to embrace your new season and get your mind in the right frame. I love the scripture that says:

> 'To everything there is a season, and a time for every matter or purpose under heaven.'
> **(Ecclesiastes 3:1, AMP)**

I feel this scripture is a reminder, if not wake-up call, of the fact that change is imminent in this journey called life. Moreover, there will be times when we don't like the change looming. Yet we have to take these steps or we stifle our growth and progress.

Now, you need to consider what changes you need to make in this season of your life. Once you have identified them, the real work then begins as you start to take the necessary action. By the way, it pays to bear in mind that you <u>do not</u> need to take this journey alone. There is a lot of help available – depending on what season you are leaving behind and which new season you are about to embrace. Do some research and see what is out there. I bet you might even discover a whole network of people, or should I say 'Bounce Back Heroes', who, having experienced a similar situation to what you are now facing, offer support to others such as yourself. What an amazing world we live in where people use their experiences to help others – a principle on which this book is based. So why not reach out to them?

Furthermore, the chances are there are other groups of people who could help, such as your friends, family, church and community, along with professionals such as coaches, mentors, counsellors and many more. So you do not have to embark on your journey alone. In fact, I would positively advise against it. I have yet to see anyone, who has achieved anything of any substance, who has done it alone. Plus the Bible states that it is always a good and wise idea to surround yourself with advisers to promote success (Proverbs 15:22). It is true to say that there is strength in numbers.

If you still feel resistant to change and need a dose of inspiration, check out the Paralympics. To me, the Paralympians represent the epitome of bouncing back. Just watching them in action is motivation for me, spurring me to keep going, no matter what I am facing. Not only did they have to overcome the hurdle of their disability, but they also subjected themselves to the strenuous training regimen required to make them the best in their chosen sport so they could qualify to represent their country in the Paralympics. What an accomplishment that is. What an even greater one when they return home with a medal or two in their clutches.

I salute them all and award them all Bounce Back Hero status, for they are deserving of it and much more.

Coach Gee says:
I believe there is a Bounce Back Hero in you. You can do whatever you set your heart to do as long as you believe all things are possible.

Adopt godly strategies

There was a time in my life when my main coping strategy was comfort eating and retail therapy. Oh, and let's not forget burying myself deep in a shedload of work. That way, I could go on ignoring the gaping wound in my heart. As long as I had my three mainstays, I thought I was coping well. In actual fact, what I was doing was simply using man-made, transient approaches to try to deal with my issues (NB: you can read more about this in my books, *Overcoming Emotional Baggage* and *Quit Hiding, Start Living!*).

Of course, these did nothing to help the challenging situation I was facing. Instead they created new ones that included a burgeoning waistline, a bulging wardrobe with items of clothing I would rarely touch, and maxed-out credit (a.k.a. debt!). So here I was, trying to keep my boat afloat with all that was going on around me. But my dodgy coping methods or behaviours were causing more problems. Why? Because they went against God's Word and ultimately left Him out of the loop.

Any approach you adopt that leaves God out of the loop or relegates Him to the backburner will end up costing you dearly. Remember, we were never created to live independently of God. Whatever we face in life, as God's children, we must bring Him into the situation.

Having had to learn this the hard way I now have a two-pronged approach which I apply to any situation I face:

Approach 1: Get God involved!

Get God involved pronto! No 'ifs' or 'buts'. The way to do this is to bring the situation to Him. Tell Him everything – how the situation has affected you, how you feel, your fears, and the like. Oh, and asking for His help, of course. By doing this, you are acknowledging God as your only source of hope whilst asserting your complete dependence on Him as the sovereign God of all the earth. Your spiritual posture is telling Him I have no one else but You. Then you cast your cares on Him, knowing fully well that He is in control. You are relinquishing control and telling Him I choose to let go and let You be God. By the way, under no circumstances are you to snatch out of His hands what you originally placed there. To me, that is just pure foolishness because in doing so you will be saying that you have no confidence in His ability. This, dear reader, is a very unwise move (ask me how I know ...).

Approach 2: Play your part

This approach is about you playing your part. Oh yes, there is a part that you must play. What I am talking about here is not passive involvement. Nah! One of your key roles is taking a stance of faith – trusting and believing that God will see you through. You also have to take the necessary action needed to achieve whatever is necessary. Have you noticed that God does not come down from Heaven to brush your teeth for you or show up at your job to do your shift for you? He has given you all you need to make the right choices and decisions for your life. In short, He has made you the CEO of Your Life Inc. So you are the one to call the shots and take action.

Within the context of unresolved issues and emotional baggage, you will need to discover what the root cause is and take steps to remedy this. The remedy may include forgiving someone, getting a counsellor, reading a book, attending a conference, training programme or retreat. You have choices.

Another action you need to take is maintaining/deepening your relationship with your heavenly Father. The last thing you want is to drift away from Him. You do this to fortify your spirit. This is accomplished through prayer, fasting, reading/meditating on God's Word, surrounding yourself with like-minded believers, and the like. I mentioned earlier that it is also wise to consider what you watch or hear because they have a tendency of taking root in your heart and germinating.

* * *

Those are the two approaches I use and I hope and pray that as you apply them, they will give you a bountiful yield.

Reflective Questions

- How do you view life or the situation you are facing? Do you typically see your cup as half empty or half full? If half empty, what can you do to change your perspective? If half full, what can you do to maintain this?
- How have you dealt with the changing seasons of your life? After reading this section, what might you consider doing differently?

- Now is a good time to consider what you have been using to *keep your boat afloat*. If you have used precarious methods, what has been the impact? What strategies would you now adopt?
- Devise your very own two-pronged approach to help you through your current season. Be specific in the actions you come up with.

Chapter Six

Develop a Bounce Back Hero Mindset

Bouncing back requires certain mindsets, which I will be covering in this chapter. The good news is that you don't have to be born with them nor do you have to come from a certain background. You can simply learn them and apply them to your life.

Keep hope alive

You might be reading this and wondering how it is possible to remain hopeful in distressing times. Your response might be, *'But you don't know what I am going or have gone through'*. Whilst I might not know the details of your situation, I am a firm believer that deep-seated hope really has nothing to do with the situation. Hope rises above this and gives one the assurance of a better future. It is the basis of the very thing we desire and look forward to, believing that things will turn out for the best in the end.

Underpin your hope with faith

Hope is underpinned by our trust in God. In the moments I find myself struggling with this, I am reminded of Hebrews 11:1 that says:

> 'Now faith is the substance of things hoped for, the evidence of things not seen.'
> **(NKJV)**

The Amplified version of this scripture says:

> 'Now faith is the assurance (the confirmation, the title deed) of the things [we] hope for, being the proof of things [we] do not see and the conviction of their reality [faith perceiving as real fact what is not revealed to the senses].'

So it is not about what we see but what we hold true in our hearts. By the way, I think I should mention at this point that remaining hopeful, as Christians, has nothing to do with the outcome we desire. We don't choose to be hopeful just because we know we will get what we want. We choose to remain hopeful, in faith, because of our confidence in a Sovereign God who holds our lives in His hands. When we do otherwise, i.e. hoping for an outcome we want, we set ourselves up for disappointment, especially when God opts for another outcome other than what we expected. For example, whilst God shows up to rescue some people, as he did in the case of Shadrach, Meshach, and Abednego, whom he saved from the burning furnace (Daniel 3), He didn't for others, who ended up tortured, suffering, or even dying for their faith. God loved both groups, and both groups of people placed their hope in God. Yet God decided their outcome, as He continues to do for all of us today. (By the way, this does not mean you should stop praying!)

One thing is certain: no one can take your hope away from you, regardless of what they may do to you. This was evident in the lives of many of the survivors and victims of the Holocaust and those of other prisoners of war. Incarcerated and living in unthinkable conditions, many of them suffered torture, starvation, cold, and much more. Yet a number managed to keep their hopes alive. In discussing his time as a hostage, Terry Waite says of his captors:

> 'You have the power to break my body, and you have tried; you have the power to bend my mind, and you have tried; but my soul is not yours to possess. There was that essential belief that my soul lay in the hands of God and couldn't be taken by others.'
>
> Source: Open House Program as heard on Hope 103.2

Life circumstances may feel like they are holding us captive. Yet we have an awesome ability to render a part of ourselves inaccessible to such captivity: our faith in

God and our hope of a better tomorrow – the latter of which culminates in our spending eternity with Him. In doing so, we can find ourselves gaining new strength and an ability to keep holding on. Waite went on to say:

> 'Don't expect God to get you out of a hole in the way that you expect. But if you have faith you will not be destroyed and you will find that you can live in hope, not just for this life but for dimensions that lie way beyond this life.'

It is always worth keeping a few points in mind:

- Life on earth is the journey we make each day towards our eternal home. When we keep this in perspective, we are able, only through God, to endure whatever hazards we experience along the way.
- Whilst we all have an idea as to how God should solve our problems and deliver us, it is futile to hold on to it inflexibly, and worse still not to give Him the room to be the creative God that He is. In doing so, we only set ourselves up for disappointment. Plus, we miss all the droplets of actions that culminate in the massive sea of miracles all around us.

Remaining hopeful is a choice

One person who typified the notion of hope was the great Austrian psychiatrist and Holocaust Survivor, Viktor Frankl. Between 1942 and 1945 he was in four Nazi death camps, including Auschwitz. In September 1942, this young doctor, his new bride, and his family were arrested in Vienna and taken to a concentration camp in Bohemia. Sadly, his parents and other members of his family died in the camps.

During and partly because of his suffering in concentration camps, the young imprisoned doctor realised the significance of meaningfulness in life. He said:

'I understood how a man who has nothing left in this world <u>still</u> may know bliss, be it only for a brief moment ...'

What a powerful statement! Unknown to Viktor, his entire family had died, with the exception of his sister. But he kept hoping to see them again. He chose to remain hopeful, despite the suffering he faced, of seeing his beloved wife again.

Viktor's powerful story reminds us that remaining hopeful, even when the fires of life engulf us, becomes a matter of choice. This links in with what you choose to see, i.e. your outlook on life. That's why I dealt with the notion of changing your perspectives earlier in the book because without this, it can seriously impede your ability to bounce back.

When I look to the Bible, one person that kept hope alive was Joseph. He was a gifted child who dreamt that his parents and brothers would some day bow down to him. Joseph naively told his father and brothers of his dream, and that, dear reader, was the beginning of the thirteen-year drama Joseph was to face before the dream came true (Genesis 37–47).

To briefly summarise Joseph's saga, it included being thrown into a pit by his brothers and then later sold into slavery. At that point, some of us might have thrown hope out of the window – we couldn't imagine being further from the dream. He arrived in Egypt and was bought by Potiphar. For a while, Joseph seemed to be doing well and was favoured by his boss who promoted him.

Then we hear of Potipher's wife taking a liking to Joseph. When he rejected her advances, she cried 'rape'. As a result, Joseph was thrown in prison. Yet even in the prison, Joseph's talent and favour made a way for him and he was again promoted. They do say you cannot keep a good man down! Here he accurately interpreted Pharaoh's baker's and his butler's dreams. Upon release, the butler, who was meant to help Joseph get out of prison, forgot about him and years passed until Pharaoh had a dream, and bingo, the butler remembered his prison chummy. Joseph was brought before Pharaoh and accurately interpreted his dreams too and even offered Pharaoh a strategy to circumvent the impending famine. As a result, Joseph was promoted to Prime Minister. Oh and yeah, his brothers did eventually bow before him.

What a drama! Every time it seemed Joseph had a break, it seemed opposing forces rose up against him. Each time he got up, he was knocked down. I often wonder what ran through his mind in those dark moments? I believe something kept him going, just as it had with David, and that was the hope of someday taking his rightful place.

We have that privilege of reading the stories of those who have gone before us. Yet none of them knew what their outcomes were going to be. They simply held on with a trust and hope in God. Today, we stand on the shoulders of these giants. Both you and I have been called, for such a time as this, to achieve a purpose. Whilst we don't know the details of the outcome, we can have a confident assurance and a hope of a good future – mapped out by God.

Coach Gee says:
'So do not throw away this confident trust in the Lord. Remember the great reward it brings you! Patient endurance is what you need now, so that you will continue to do God's will. Then you will receive all that he has promised.' (Hebrews 10:35–36, NLT)

Move beyond the pain

Have you ever had a painful experience that you simply can't get over? How can you tell if you are caught in this trap? Let me use a personal experience of mine to highlight the point. Ironically, in this situation, Father used a complete stranger (possibly an unbeliever) to bring home the fact that I had a tendency to dwell on my pain and suffering.

The journey from hell

Some years back I enrolled on a one-day training course and was so excited that I'd be attending. However, the excitement was soon dampened by the not-so-useful joining and travel instructions sent ahead of the event. They were really poor. Normally I am super-organised, and plan everything to within an inch of its life. I have a contingency plan, just in case, which means I usually arrive way ahead of time. I hate being late as it unsettles me, and I have been known to arrive at speaking engagements even before the doors opened!

Anyway, back to my story ...

On this occasion, I had left home in good time and my satellite navigator promptly announced, *'You have now arrived at your destination'*. Huh? I thought. Despite using the postcode provided, there was nowhere that resembled a training facility. Instead, I was faced with a gated residential community! Arrrgggghh! I thought. I decided to press the gate intercom: perhaps someone could direct me. To do this I had to step out of the car. The moment I did, the Heavens opened. You can imagine my frustration when a voice came through the intercom and told me that although I was near the venue, this was not the right entrance. They then tried to give me instructions, but with the noise of the rain and the busy dual carriageway behind me I could barely hear them.

I backed out of the driveway and returned to the one-way busy dual carriageway despite the pleas of my trusted navigator who kept telling me to turn back. Do a U-turn on a one-way dual carriageway? Not on your life! So I followed the road, which was getting busier and slowing down because of the rain. Then the navigator suggested I came off at the next exit and follow a convoluted series of roads just to get to the other side of the dual carriageway. I followed dutifully and joined the dual carriageway when I was told to. Finally, I felt like I was back on track. I still had 50 minutes before start-time and I was near the venue. I had planned to arrive an hour before the event and thank God I had because what happened next was enough to blow anyone's fuse.

Arriving at a roundabout, both myself and the satellite navigator were confused. Where were we supposed to go now? Being a tad hesitant sparked the odd horn from other drivers. I could just hear them say, *'Women drivers, huh!'* Not sure where I was to go and with no decent road signs, I took the exit I thought must be the right one. And guess what, I was back on the same one-way dual carriageway I had been on fifteen minutes earlier. Whilst I don't curse, on that day I was close to doing so. So here I was on that same stretch of road and I had to travel to the next exit, go down the long convoluted roads, get back on the road the opposite side and start again. Once more I had to make a decision as to what exit to take. At the time, I thought the only two options in front of me would either take me back home or further from where I thought the venue was.

And so I found myself ... you guessed right, on that one-way dual carriageway. This happened a total of three times, and on the fourth attempt I decided to take a random exit, one which just felt so wrong. By this point

I was soaked, tired, frustrated and just wanted to go home (another 120 mile hike). Sadly, there was nowhere to stop and no one to ask. I had tried to call the company that was hosting the event but no one was available. Seemed like being early was not their thing, as I would have expected them to be at the venue at least thirty minutes before the event. I guess that was too much to ask.

Eventually, I managed to get through to someone. I then explained where I was and they gave me directions. Trust me, even a seasoned driver or the most up-to-date satellite navigator would have struggled, because even with those vague directions there were no road signs to what turned out to be a very large business industrial estate.

Eventually I arrived at another entrance to the large industrial estate and there were no signs to the actual building that housed the training venue. I was huffing and puffing by then. When I asked the security guards at the gate where the building was one of them took a shine to me and I thought, *'Don't even go there. I am not in the mood!'* His colleague gave me some long, drawn-out directions. Little did I know I would spend another ten minutes or so looking for this building within the estate that had no signs. After having had to drive in heavy rain and spending so long looking for the venue I had by now run out of steam, so I plonked the car in a carpark I had seen a few people heading for. The plan was to see where they went. By now, the course would have started as my one-hour buffer had been exhausted.

So I walked into a building and I saw a group of people waiting. I asked if they were here for the course and they said yes. Phew! FINALLY! Wet, makeup a mess, with a mass of hair that no longer looked as stylish as when I had first set out that morning, I knew a storm was brewing within me, with a not-so-good attitude in tow. I struck up a conversation with a young lady – a fellow attendee – and told her about my drama-filled journey. And you know what her simple answer was?

'But you are here now'.

WHAT? Had she not heard what I'd just said? Did she not see that the whole saga had upset me? How could she just say that? I was peeved with her because I expected a little sympathy at the very least. Instead, it felt like she had belittled my painful journey.

Don't dwell on the pain

When I later reflected on my painful journey that day and that young lady's response, it became clear to me that Father was speaking directly to me. He was saying, *'But you are here now'*.

You see, like many people who have endured a painful experience or a time of suffering, I had a tendency to dwell on or relive bad experiences. But each time we recall an experience, we drag up with it the negative emotions we attached to those memories. That's why you may observe that when you remember a particular experience, you might notice your heart rate increasing; you talk louder and/or faster; you gesticulate and find yourself getting agitated – pretty much the way you did when you'd had that experience. You may even find your blood pressure and stress hormones increase. What's happening here is that you are reliving the moment even though it was in the past. You are responding physically, physiologically and emotionally.

When we don't effectively deal with our experiences, such as getting help to overcome the trauma of them, it becomes challenging to detach the unhealthy negative emotions we associate with those experiences. However, although we simply cannot delete the memory, as we would a file on our computers, we can learn to tell our stories and recall events without the unhealthy negative emotions surfacing. This is when you know you have moved beyond your pain.

At the time, I did not realise I was harbouring a resentment towards the event organisers. And I don't think my tending towards super-efficiency or perfectionism helped matters. But thankfully today I can recount the nightmare journey with a smile on my face thinking, *'Chill out, Gladys!'*

You would have thought that after that experience I would have learnt my lesson. Well, let's just say I needed to retake the 'Don't Dwell on your Pain 101' module again. I did say this was a journey and we grow over time. Though I do see changes in myself, I am not there yet.

For example, I was recently telling someone how hard it was to complete my second Masters degree. I did an MA in Publishing and studied full time. My gosh, that was a challenge and a half! I have fond memories (well <u>not</u> quite fond memories, if the truth be told) of staying all night in the library trying to write essays or complete assignments. And as for the dissertation, I never thought anything could be so hard. For a period of three months or so, sleep became of past luxury! As I told the story, I could just hear Father whisper, *'But you are here now'*. And indeed I was. Not only that, but the dissertation that was so arduous to complete and robbed me of my sleep was awarded best project in the UK and I came out top of my class for the year! By the time I had completed the course I had ended up winning three separate awards and prizes!

Notwithstanding, I still referred back to the pain. That was, until I got the revelation that, in essence, we are what we focus on. Whatever I choose to focus on today I am allowing to take root. Remember Proverbs 23:7, which I mentioned previously? It says:

'For as he thinks in his heart, so is he.'
(NKJ)

So was it any surprise that all I was reminded of today were the painful memories I sowed yesterday? With this in mind, I now needed to change my thinking. I needed to change how I positioned my experiences. I needed to change the focus and stop dwelling on the negative aspect of each experience. I needed to move away from the unhealthy negative emotions provoked by an unhealthy or irrational belief about the experience. I also needed to (re)learn how to recall the story in a positive way and not dwell solely on the 'bad' bits.

No matter what we face there is always something positive to bring out of the experience. Our challenge is what we choose to focus on. Agreed, it may have been a challenging experience that caused trauma. But the Bible, and more recent research, still indicates that the challenging life experience can become a catalyst for positive change and growth. Our bad/ugly journeys in life do not have to render us dysfunctional.

Stephen Joseph, Ph.D., author of the book, *What Doesn't Kill Us: The New Psychology of Posttraumatic Growth*, states that:

> 'The field of psychological trauma is changing as researchers recognise that adversity does not always lead to a damaged and dysfunctional life. Post-traumatic growth refers to how adversity can be a springboard to higher levels of psychological well-being.'

Therefore, the lesson here is to leverage our experiences and use them as a springboard – aligned with what God may have us do – to leap into the dawn of a new season in our lives.

Lastly, I have come to the conclusion that whilst we remain resolutely focused on the negative aspects of an experience, with unhealthy negative emotions in tow, we become unable to celebrate our victories, including all the positive aspects of that same experience. Furthermore, we may well not be thanking God for getting us through. Why? Because we cannot see the wood for the trees!

Over the years I have come to realise that, for some people, this cycle does not stop even when they go on achieve great levels of success. They can still find these negative emotions tending to obscure their achievements, and they may leave them susceptible to feeling unfulfilled or feeling like a failure. That's why it is important to weed out any potential hindrances now. One way of doing this is constantly checking your attitudes and belief systems to ensure they are aligned with God's Word.

If your dream is big enough, the facts simply don't count!

Following on from moving beyond the pain, the next step is all about looking ahead and dreaming of a better tomorrow. You can achieve this by having a dream or a goal to hold on to. By the way, having a dream or a hope of a better future has nothing to do with your current circumstances. Dr Munroe says:

> 'If you have hope for the future you have true riches; no matter how much you have in your account.'

I think Samina's story will encourage you to believe it.

The power of a mother's dream

Samina was raised in a remote village in India. At fourteen, her parents arranged a marriage for her to a man she did not know. She then left her village and started her new life in Kolkata. Being poor, they squatted in an abandoned horse stable in the middle of Mollahati slum. The slum had 10,000 people, one tap and two toilets!

Sadly, the newly married couple were poor and her husband, Rabiul, had irregular work carrying bricks on construction sites. Often the family went to bed with nothing more than water in their stomachs.

Within a year of getting married, she became pregnant and had a son, Jane' Alam. But they had no money at all to provide properly for their son's needs. Samina said, *'Every parent wants to give their child good things but we could not do that because we had no money'*. Each day, Samina would see children go to school in their smart uniforms. And she started dreaming of the day her son would be educated and be able to make a difference. That became the dream she held on to, though the reality was that they could never make this happen. In spite of that, she carried her dream with her.

Luckily for her son Jane' Alam, he got a sponsor when his father registered him in a Compassion project at his local church. Compassion, an international Christian child development and child advocacy organisation, is committed to the spiritual, economic, social and physical development of children living in extreme poverty in 26 countries, enabling them to become responsible, fulfilled Christian adults. Through Jane' Alam's sponsor, he was able to get food, clothes, education and much more. Interestingly, Jane' Alam was the first in his community to go to school.

As you can imagine, Samina was overjoyed. To her amazement someone was actually helping them make their dream come true. The burden was off their shoulders. Jane' Alam went on to do exceedingly well in his education. He was top of his class in high school and went on to obtain a bachelor's degree, coming second out of 1,500 students. Jane' Alam became a great asset to his family, supporting them financially and helping with the education of his sister.

Later, Jane' Alam went on to obtain a Masters in Business Administration from Manchester University in England. Determined to share his opportunities with those from his community when he finished school, he began working with a micro finance project to help prostitutes find alternatives for survival. Now, he is setting up *Pursuit* – an organisation with a vision to see people trapped in physical and spiritual poverty empowered to pursue a life of hope and purpose. He is using his business acumen to raise funds in support of a whole portfolio of projects to support more people from his home community.

Samina says:

'I feel very proud. Many people dream but I have now realised my dream. There are so many kids in Kolkata but my son, with his background, has achieved so much. It makes me proud to be a mum'.

Samina's story reminds me of a quote by Dr Myles Munroe, from his book, *Releasing your Potential: Exposing the Hidden You*, which says:

'Every human heart cries and yearns for the same thing: a chance to fulfil his or her own dreams and desires. Even the poorest man has a dream.'

Samina had a dream despite her circumstances. And she went on to prove that if the dream is big enough, the facts truly don't count! Agreed, they were poor, lived in a slum and had no chance of educating their child. Yet they were undeterred and held on to the dream. And through divine intervention and nothing short of a miracle they got the support they needed through an amazing organisation. I am sure we have not heard the end of Jane' Alam's achievements.

So perhaps it is time for you to start dreaming again, if you have not done so. Dr Munroe goes onto say:

'The poorest person in the world is the person without a dream.'

Don't let your experiences in life deter you. Whilst you might be in the midst of adversity, suffering or trauma, you can still hold on to a dream or goal. Don't worry about how it will happen. Your job right now is to incubate your dream, in faith, hoping for a day it will materialise.

One dream or goal you may want to set for yourself is how you could use your life experiences, coupled with your gifts/skills, to make a positive difference in someone else's life. Now is the time to prayerfully consider what Father would have you do as a result of your experiences. It is likely He has use for what is in your hands. So use this opportunity to find out what you have to offer the world. Trust me, you have loads to offer.

Coach Gee says:

Your experiences + your skills/talent = a candidate who can make a positive difference in the world. So dream big and go for it.

God always has a plan

The Bible tells us God has a plan for each of our lives. Jeremiah 29:11 says:

> 'For I know the plans I have for you," says the Lord. "They are plans for good and not for disaster, to give you a future and a hope.'
>
> (NLT)

How exciting to know that like Queen Esther, we are all born for such a time as this, to fulfil God's plans here on earth. God must have thought, 'I need _____ (fill in the gap with your name) to help Me in achieving *ABC* or *XYZ*.' And so He orchestrated that you would be born at a certain time and place so as to fulfil His plans. But not only that: He knew you would need a particular skill, talent or experience to assist with that. He also knew that certain character traits would support you in your role. So He made everything work together.

If you were to take a moment to reflect, you might notice that you have one or more skill sets or talents. Or perhaps your journey thus far sets you apart from others. Whatever is the case, you have been set up for greatness and all that you need is already inside you. It is within your reach. Our challenge today is keeping this in mind as we navigate through life.

Another great thing about the scripture in Jeremiah 29:11 is that it reassures and reaffirms us. Personally, the scripture has brought me comfort on many occasions, especially when I have what I call my *Joseph moments* where it seems my present reality could not be any further from the hopes, dreams and promises I incubate on the inside. Reading the scripture, over and over, gives me a confident hope that even in the midst of life's dramas there is a godly scheme working itself out for me. And that, dear reader, acts in a similar way on me as a pacifier would on a baby.

In fact, when life does not make sense at all I have learnt to adopt King David's stance on such matters, though it may take me a little while to get there. Paraphrasing Psalms 131, I don't get bogged down with the detail. Looking at verse 1 and 2, it says:

> '... I don't concern myself with matters too
> great or too awesome for me to grasp.
> Instead, I have calmed and quieted myself, like a
> weaned child who no longer cries for its mother's milk.
> Yes, like a weaned child is my soul within me.'
> **(NLT)**

When I get caught up in my 'why' moments I tend to feel overwhelmed. No surprises there, as 1) that's not my concern and 2) my shoulders were never designed to carry such burdens. That's God's business! I simply have to follow Him in obedience and fix my gaze heavenward – even though a tsunami-type wave is about to hit me. Though I might be jittery, I know I can run to God.

Coach Gee says:
Meditate on the scripture in Jeremiah 29:11 and let it sink into your spirit.

Reflective Questions

- What positive steps can you take today to keep your hope alive even in difficult times? Some ideas include:
  o Reminding yourself of God's ability
  o Meditating on God's Word
  o Having a dream, purpose or goal
  o Reading/listening/watching uplifting content
  o Hanging out with people (e.g. friends and family) who can encourage you
  o Speaking to someone such as a counsellor, pastor, etc.

- Do you find yourself struggling with past hurts and/or forgiving others? Below are two resources that can help:

- *Quit Hiding Start Living! How Women Can Free Themselves from Past Hurts* (Gladys Famoriyo)
- *Extending the Olive Branch: Forgiveness as Healing* (Sharon Platt-McDonald)

Part III – Maximising

Turning Your Trials into Triumphs

Chapter Seven

Don't Waste Your Pain!

Whilst you might think the notion of wasting one's pain may seem absurd, it is actually possible. As you may have gathered by now, a number of people have been able to channel their adversity, trauma or challenging life situation into something positive. They have used it as a springboard to transform various aspects of their lives and those of others. These individuals chose not to waste the experience and/or let it get the better of them. Somehow they were able to overcome their situation whilst creating a new meaning or purpose for their lives.

Following the suicide of his son, Rick Warren, who wrote the bestselling book, *The Purpose Driven Life*, says:

'... Sadly, most people squander their suffering, don't profit from their problems, never learn from their losses and are unable to advance from their adversity or gain from their pain. Don't waste your pain; let God heal it, recycle it, utilize it and use it to bless other people.'

And so we will continue the journey looking at how you can use your experiences in an effective way.

Maximise your waiting room experience

We all know that time flies. If we don't take care of the fleeting moments in life, we may wake one day to discover that it's all over. I believe John Ortberg's awesome book, aptly titled *'When the Game is Over, it All Goes Back in the Box'*, was written to help people develop a better game plan for their lives – one with a focus on eternity.

One of the key lessons I learnt from the book was to always focus on what really matters the most. Once clear on this, we need to decide to use our time wisely lest we spend our lives chasing the wrong things. Whether we like it or not, the truth is we are all enrolled in the game called 'life' and have tasks to do. But we still need a game plan or else we find ourselves wasting our lives.

Use your time wisely

Have you ever stopped to observe people in the waiting room of their dentist's or doctor's surgery? I have, and I have come to see those differences as a good illustration of how people use their time.

There are those who do nothing. When I say nothing, I mean nothing! They fold their hands, stare into space and seem to zone out. We will call them Group A. Then there are those who spend their time flicking through the out-dated magazines, reading pamphlets, or watching the digital displays. I will refer to these as Group B. Lastly, there are those who come prepared, knowing they will most likely have to wait. And so out comes the book or smart phone to catch up on emails, social media or play a game. These are Group C.

My goal here is not to pronounce that one of the three groups uses their time better than the others, as the person sitting doing nothing may be enjoying a rare moment of peace, and the person on the phone might be more in need of taking a chill-pill. Rather than taking a literal approach, I want to reflect on these metaphorically.

Whilst there are many ways to view this metaphor, I would like you to see the waiting room as one that represents challenging life experience. At some point, your name will be called and you get to leave the room. But, for now, you are here. Using the same groupings as before, the Group A individuals may be comprised of two subgroups: those who find themselves sitting still for a reason, quite possibly because of their situation (e.g. illness, trauma, etc.); and those who, after experiencing their 'life' moment, could be finding themselves stuck. For both groups, time will tell what their next step will be. Those in the first, however, who have a Bounce Back mindset, will find that although their immediate situation is likely to require rest, and a need to incorporate the 5Rs, when they get back on their feet they will typically bounce back from the experience or setback. They may have even used part of their time thinking about how they can make something positive out of their experience.

Group B individuals may want to use their time in the waiting room constructively but are unprepared to do so. This is either because they don't know how to do this or have no idea of what they could be doing productively. They may end up taking a stab at one thing or another but it is neither fulfilling nor do they have the passion for it. Having no real focus most likely results in chasing other people's dreams or goals – ones that do not align with their purpose. However, by embracing a Bounce Back mindset, they can start to find a meaning or purpose for their experiences and talents. In doing so, the game plan they create becomes aligned with these.

Lastly for our Group C folks, although they are active it's worth considering on what they are expending their efforts and how they are using their time. I think it is safe to say not all busyness is profitable, and not all periods of stillness are wasted. The waiting room affords potential Bounce Back Heroes to not only plan for what's next but also to pause, reflect and listen. Is this God's game plan for them? Might He have another plan for them? Once clear on what's next, they can progress ahead.

Waiting for the right time?!?!

I want to mention at this juncture that I honestly don't believe we need to wait till we have all our ducks lined up in a row before we take action. We don't have to wait till we have it all figured out, have the money etc. before we make progress. It's all about using the time you have wisely. When we fold our arms, waiting for the storm to pass or waiting for more favourable conditions, we become like the farmers depicted in Ecclesiastes 11:4:

> *'Farmers who wait for perfect weather never plant.*
> *If they watch every cloud, they never harvest.'*
> (NLT)

The challenge we face is knowing when to move or not. I am all for the notion of divine timing and recognise there is an appointed season for everything under the sun. Farmers know the correct window of time to plant their crops. When I buy plant seeds, there are always suggestions on the packaging as to when the best time of the year is to plant them. The same goes for us. There is a time for us to launch our project or plan – which could be before, during or after our 'waiting room' experiences. Dear reader, there is only one way to find out, and that is by consulting the One who sent you here in the first place. After all, He has the blueprint of your life. Just ask. This was what Ruth, a client of mine, did. Here is her story:

Ruth was diagnosed with Lupus about 19 years ago. In her own words, she felt like she had been given a death sentence, as the prognosis was not great. Thanks to advances in science and the treatment of Lupus, sufferers could live beyond the five-year mark though it continues to remain a life-threatening illness. The ensuing years, for Ruth, were filled with many highs, but equally many lows, owing to her Lupus flare-ups.

Prior to my getting to know Ruth, she had attended two of our ministry events in London: The annual Overcoming Emotional Baggage (OEB) Women's Conference and our OEB Ambassador Training Programme. It was through the latter that I got to know her. So it was really sad to discover that shortly after the training course she had experienced a really bad flare of Lupus and was now in hospital. Upon hearing the news, I touched base with her whilst rallying the ministry team to include her in our daily and weekly prayers. This latest flare up was to become a poignant waiting-room experience for Ruth.

Firstly, Ruth had decided from the onset that this flare up, unlike the others, was not going to keep her down. Secondly, she decided to turn to God and use the experience to deepen her relationship with Him. This was a task in itself as she was often exhausted and spent most of her time in bed. Yet, in what seemed like a dark period of her life, Ruth became very aware of her other task for the season: she was to write a book. She had felt the nudge to write for some time and it became clear now that this was the appointed time.

And so, while off her feet, off work, and in bed, Ruth started to write her devotionals. That's when she came to me as a client. As her book coach/consultant, we worked around her condition to achieve her goal of publishing her first devotional. As I write, Ruth's completed manuscript has been submitted to her publisher. I am pleased to say her book will be published sometime before the end of summer this year.

But it was not all plain sailing. In between the writing and shortly before our next ministry event – our annual OEB women's weekend retreat – she suffered yet another health setback, which meant she was back in hospital. Not only that, the flare up was so bad, she now had to relearn how to walk! Yet Ruth remained determined to the point whereby she left the hospital the night before the retreat started and headed there the following morning. She arrived at the reception of the retreat venue on a mobility scooter, owing to the limited use of her legs. Interestingly enough, it packed up as soon as she arrived at the reception! I fondly recall Ruth asking me to pray for her scooter and I laughed. I told her God has a sense of humour and that I had a feeling He had no use for the scooter over the weekend (and neither did she)!

Needless to say, Ruth left the weekend retreat with full use of her legs. If I remember correctly, she could not stop skipping and jumping all weekend long after we had all witnessed her healing miracle, right before our very eyes, during the first worship/prayer session! Her physiotherapist, who saw her the following week, was speechless. He simply wrote in her notes, *walking miracle*! All through her illness episodes Ruth was never deterred. She maxed out her waiting-room time and was ready to conquer the world when it was her time to leave. For that, she deserves a Bounce Back Hero award!

Coach Gee says:
Why not spend some time today praying to get divine guidance on what you should be doing with your waiting-room time.

Feel the pain but do it anyway!

This is exactly what my dear friend Sharon did. Let me tell you a little bit about her. We met some years ago at the Christian Resources Exhibition and we simply clicked. We became like sisters and often prayed together, laughed and cried. She also became my 'partner in crime' when it came to my ministry's OEB conferences and retreats. She is one powerful 'chick' with a passion for God and a drive to see people healed holistically. She has written several books, produced resources, including manuals, programmes, videos, and so much more. Sharon is the epitome of someone whose gift 'tap' never gets turned off just because life happened. She just keeps pouring out and overflowing into those around her.

So Sharon's response to the incident I am about to share *really* did not surprise me.

It's raining suitcases!

A few days after our 2011 OEB Women's Conference, Sharon boarded a plane headed for Montenegro, where she was scheduled to preach for five days. As she sat down in her seat a most unfortunate incident occurred.

In his efforts to get the passengers ready for take-off, a flight attendant over-packed the overhead bin closest to Sharon. He tried five times to close it after he had squeezed in a late arriving passenger's luggage. Though there were a number of other empty overhead bins, seeing it was not a full flight, the flight attendant persisted in squeezing in this last bag.

Unfortunately for Sharon, a heavy, oversized hard luggage case fell with full force on her head! When the suitcase fell, Sharon was thrown forward into the seat in front, then backwards and then into the middle again which meant her brain rocked in her skull 3 times! In that moment, she feared some serious damage had been done (she has a background in nursing and midwifery). Whizzing through her mind was what might be the extent of the injury and whether she would be able to preach for five days.

Furthermore, Sharon had as a reference point two women who recently had head injuries. Sadly, one died and Sharon had attended her funeral. The other lady had a brain haemorrhage and a blood clot requiring brain surgery but through the grace of God, she survived. However, her life was changed dramatically and she now lives with family members where previously she lived alone. With this in mind, Sharon feared the worse.

To ease the pain and swelling, she was given a cooling pack for her head. She then prayed Father would keep her till her assignment was done in Montenegro. And so He did. The moment she arrived back in the UK, her health deteriorated and she was rushed to hospital.

She was struggling with her speech and at some point lost consciousness. She was diagnosed with protracted post-concussion syndrome and, as a result, Sharon, who was the Director of three departments, Women, Health and Disability, for the Adventist Church (UK & British Isles), could not work for six months and worked from home for a year. Her speech remained impaired and she had difficulty staying awake for periods of the day. Along with that came all sorts of hospital appointments, including speech therapy, and it didn't help that she was declared unfit to drive. She had to cancel several key engagements and put on hold others for an indefinite time.

When I visited Sharon, my heart went out to her though she was very much full of 'beans'. Her speech was returning (though still slurred) and she was able to stay awake for longer periods at a time. As a result of the accident, her life was on hold; she now had to contend with the fact that she might never be able to function normally again. This included both her writing and her speaking engagements.

Like most of us who have been through a life trauma like this, Sharon wondered why it was happening to her, and why now. Dare I say, she also had her share of spiritual fits and holy tantrums. Why did this have to happen to her just when she was doing so much work for the kingdom and changing lives. Was she now to walk away from all of this?

Yet in her 'waiting-room' experience, something beautiful happened. Whilst battling with speech problems and drowsy episodes, Sharon used her times of consciousness and inability to fully communicate to put together a women's devotional entitled *Light On The Path, Volume 1*, to encourage women in times when life leaves you scratching your head, those times when you are made to think, 'huh?'.

It has been three-and-a-half years, and during this time Sharon has had to have speech therapy as she continues to have speech deficits when she is tired or stressed. She has not been allowed to drive yet (under medical advice) as she still suffers from drowsy episodes as a result of the head injury.

Despite all this, I am glad to say there have been more books and resources since then. To me, Sharon will forever be an inspiration and I am awarding her the status of lifetime Bounce Back Hero. Why? Because many other 'life' moments have cropped up since then but like the energiser bunny in the battery advert, she keeps going on and on and on – never seemingly phased by life. Her positive attitude in the face of her experiences was a driver for writing this book. Some people would have walked away from God and their calling after experiencing a fraction of what she has gone through. I have seen people do this. Yet she remains a stalwart for God. I salute you Shaz!

In closing, you may argue as to why God would allow all this stuff to happen to someone who is obviously doing great things. Remember, as I mentioned earlier, it's all about your perspectives in life.

To bounce back, I take the standpoint that 1) God knows what He is doing, 2) God is still in charge and 3) we have a promise in Romans 8:28 that He works out *everything* for our good! Moreover, the waiting room is the opportune place to become malleable – allowing God to help us to adapt to the situation or season – so we do not need to switch the 'taps' of our gifts off. Moreover, so we can survive, thrive and maximise our transient moments on Earth.

God can use you even when down

In my faith walk, I have come to realise that we all have a mandate in our lives to carry out what I call Kingdom Business. I don't believe this mandate needs to be thrown out of the window or that we should abdicate our calling just because life happens. Through my own experiences, I have found that even in the midst of pain, if I yield myself, Father can still use me to touch the lives of others.

I have to say I balked at the idea at first, as if to say to God, *'You can't be serious. Can't You see what's going on with me? I need help too!'* I have come to realise, though, that God wasn't being horrible or insensitive to my plight or personal needs. And when I stopped feeling sorry for myself, I could resume seeing the bigger picture and God's plan for humanity, one which I am part of. And there have been plenty of times when, although stuff was going on in my backyard, I had clear instructions and nudge to achieve a particular task.

For example, there have been times when I felt Him ask me to reach out to others, despite my own need. In obedience, I have given money when I was short myself.

I have encouraged others with texts, cards, calls or a visit at times I could have done with the same. I have lost count of all the heavenly 'nudges' I have had through the years. Yet, when I conformed, the recipients have always been deeply touched (to say the least). On most occasions, they have confided in me that what they received was answer to an inward prayer or desperate need. And that fact that God will stop what He was doing, hear their cries and orchestrate someone, somewhere to meet that need, fills them with indescribable joy. And as a result, their faith in God grows. The gesture becomes a lovely reminder that they are on Father's mind and they are loved.

I remember the period when I wrote my third book, *Healing a Discouraged Heart: Getting Back on Track When Life Lets You Down*, I was grieving the loss of my Dad. Whilst I did not feel like writing and I was really struggling with grief and discouragement, I started writing because I felt a nudge to do so. Plus, I had questions of my own that needed answering. So I continued to write. If I am honest, that was one of the hardest things I've had to do. Often, tears would roll down my face – partly because of the grief I was experiencing and partly because I could feel Father gradually propelling me out of the chasm of discouragement into which I had wedged myself. But as I continued to write, I started to see a glimmer of hope – one I had not seen for a while.

With His grace, strength and direction, the manuscript for *Healing a Discouraged Heart* was completed and published. But the story did not end there. I started getting feedback and testimonials from discouraged people who were growing weary in their Christian walk. They too had prayed, hoped and waited and nothing seemed to be happening. One moving yet simple email that came through from one lady simply said:

> 'Thank you Gladys for writing Healing a Discouraged Heart. Since reading it, there have been fewer tears'.

Wow! Who would have thought that a simple act of obedience <u>during</u> (not after) a very difficult time in my life would help someone else on his or her journey?

Over the years, I have moved away from resenting the heavenly 'nudges' as I have come to realise it all forms part of God's Kingdom Business. Now, I consider it a privilege to be a cog in God's wheel (a very small one, might I add) to bring a smile to someone's face, encourage someone on their journey, or offer them hope.

The flip side of this is that when we choose to withhold, and ignore God's 'nudges', someone somewhere may suffer as a result. It is not to say God is not able to find another willing vessel. He is more than able. But He chose you and me to do His bidding, despite the distress in our own lives. It is always worth remembering that when we are weak, we are actually strong (2 Corinthians 13:9). Furthermore, we go in His strength (Psalm 71:16, NKJV) and He gives us the desire and power to do it – as Philippians 2: 13 says:

> 'For God is working in you, giving you the desire and the power to do what pleases him.'
> **(NLT)**

'*[Not in your own strength] for it is God Who is all the while effectually at work in you [energizing and creating in you the power and desire], both to will and to work for His good pleasure and satisfaction and delight.*'

(AMP)

Coach Gee says:
When you yield yourself to God, it is amazing how He can turn what seems like your weak moments into something great. Your role in all of this is to yield to His nudge and He will do the rest.

Listen to your life!

As much as I may bemoan tough times, if I am really honest, many of those times became my wake-up call. In those times, I have experienced personal, professional and spiritual growth spurts. My waiting-room days became the rare moments I could experience the 5Rs – rest, recover, replenish, reflect and regroup. It is during these periods I often feel closer to God. With no distractions to hand, He has my full attention. I may get instructions for the next season; I may even get to see how I have veered from my path of purpose. But one thing is for sure, I am repositioned, because life seems to be saying, '*hello Gladys, this is your life calling. Wake up! This is no rehearsal!*'

Hello, this is your life calling

The night I got a phone call from my sister to say my dear father had passed away, I instantly knew it was a wake-up call. Up to that point, I had never lost anyone close, and that episode rocked the foundations of my world and, dare I say, my faith. Dad's passing raised a number of unresolved issues for me, which included my unvoiced issues about death and my lack of forgiveness towards Dad. I had a dark cloud hanging over me and my outlook on life was not great.

My initial response in the waiting room was to fold my arms in anger and bitterness, refusing to budge. I even stopped praying, reading my Bible, and going to church! That period was my lowest point. But, over time, I experienced inner healing and I moved from Group A, then to B, and finally to C. But not without the prayers and encouragement of family and friends. And it was during that same period that my book, *Healing a Discouraged Heart*, was conceived.

Dad's passing taught me a valuable lesson: maximise every day because none of us knows when our time will be up. The experience awakened a new strength, and the desire to max out my God-given talents and live a life of no regrets.

So I started writing with fervour, as I had so many book ideas, as well as some half-written and others ready to be published. It took Dad's passing for me to realise I was sitting on a goldmine. And if care was not taken, life would fly by, and I'd wake up when it was too late. I even went back to university full time and did an MA in Publishing.

The ensuing books I wrote and published gave me a platform to speak to thousands of people (nationally and internationally), to be interviewed on TV and radio, and to launch a ministry. I also started a women's academy, the Gladys Famoriyo Academy, aimed at nurturing and developing other female authors, leaders and speakers. The goal was to offer expert advice, drawing from my experiences, and much more.

I could go on here but I think you get the gist. Something happened when I got that wake-up call and I embraced it with both arms. So whilst I miss Dad dearly, his legacy of fully embracing life and persistently venturing into the unknown continues to spur me on, and gave me a virtual kick up the rear end when I needed it.

Let life's knocks propel you forward

I have noticed that our 'life' moments have a tendency of developing empathy in us towards others going through similar experiences. Until I lost Dad, I really could not relate with those who were experiencing grief. Until I was unwell, I really could not understand what it felt like for one's body not to function the way it was designed to work. Whilst you can give people a hug, comfort them, perform acts of kindness; you *really* don't know what they are going through unless you have walked a mile in their shoes.

Am I saying the only way to develop compassion, etc., is experiencing the situation yourself? Not necessarily! Parents caring for a child diagnosed with a rare condition, or family/friends who watch someone they know experience a challenging ordeal can develop it too, just as Dela did with her brother Tayo who had kidney failure.

So regardless of whether the situation happened to you or someone else, I have noticed that it does something to the human heart. More often than not, it pulls on our heartstrings and the result is passion and compassion coming together. This is what mobilises us as humans to achieve great feats in an effort to bring relief to others. In fact, there are many people volunteering, running marathons and jumping out of planes to support a charity or cause they are passionate about. Not all of these people have been through the experience themselves but they have developed a real compassion for their cause. Last year, I ran the Race for Life 10k run for Cancer Research UK as I wanted to support their great efforts. Through the grace of God, I have not had (and hopefully will not have) a brush with cancer. Yet I continue to support such causes.

This is the drive that underpins people, who, after experiencing their 'life' moment, go off and launch a charity, campaign, programme, or even dedicate their lives to helping others. What they have done is used their experiences as a springboard to great accomplishments, using the new opportunity their experience afforded them. Many, like Zoe and Sharon whom I mentioned earlier, simply feel compelled to do this. And when they come out the other side of their experience (or before, in the case of Sharon and Ruth), resilient as ever, they wear their Bounce Back hero outfits and go off and use their trauma to transform those dramas in the lives of others.

Coach Gee says:
Ponder on the scripture in Psalm 90:12 that says, *'So teach us to number our days, that we may gain a heart of wisdom.'* (NKJV). Take heed ... the clock is ticking.

Reflective Questions

- Using the waiting-room scenario, in which group do you see yourself – A, B or C? What can you start to do to ensure you maximise your waiting-room experience?
- After reading Sharon and Ruth's story, are there any lessons you can learn? What might you start, stop or continue to do so as not to waste your pain?
- Is there something you can do today for someone to bring a smile to their face or bring a ray of sunshine into their world?
- Take a moment to ponder on this question: Is your life trying to tell you something? Make a note of whatever lessons it may be trying to teach you.

Chapter Eight

Reinvent Your Purpose

One thing is for sure: we all have a purpose in life and people's responses to it vary. Some grab it with both hands; others think, *'no thanks ... not for me'*, and everyone else fits somewhere between these two reactions.

Whilst researching for this book, something became apparent: life's challenging moments have a way of changing how we see it and the roles we ultimately play. If you have not given this much thought prior to your 'life' moment, it is very likely the jolt will cause you to think (if not act) on how you might be able to use your experiences. My personal 'jolts' got me back on track, especially with writing, at the point I had veered off it. I have noticed that other people too find a (re)new purpose or meaning for their lives. This chapter helps you consider how to use the remainder of your time.

Create a meaning for your life

When creating a meaning of your life, there are two areas I would like you to consider. One focuses on creating a vision for the future; the other on what's in your hands.

Have a vision for the future

Earlier on, I mentioned the plight of Viktor Frankel, the Holocaust survivor. In his time in the concentration camp he noticed that, among those given a chance for survival, it was the ones who held on to a vision of the future – whether it was a significant task or a return to their loved ones – who were the most likely to survive. In his book, *Man's Search for Meaning*, Frankl said:

> 'There is nothing in the world, I venture to say, that would so effectively help one to survive even the worst conditions as the knowledge that there is a meaning in one's life.'

This deep insight resonates to the core of human beings. By holding on to a vision of the future, it has the power to keep us focused and hopeful, even if our present situation is dire. When we deeply believe in that vision, it's as if a picture of it has been permanently etched into our hearts. Hidden deep within us, this can never be taken away from us, even in the face of torture and suffering, as the Christians of old found who refused to deny Christ. No one can take this vision and hope away from us though many have tried. Frankl went on to agree with philosopher Friedrich Nietzsche who said:

'He who has a why to live for can bear with almost any how.'

I believe this was the same mindset that propelled Nelson Mandela who, despite his long battle for freedom, which included imprisonment for 27 years, refused to be broken, even under the most trying of circumstances. His life was a picture of courage, persistence and, most of all, forgiveness. Despite the poor conditions of prison life he held on to the hope of a better day. Although he was behind bars, his fight for freedom never stopped. And when he was offered freedom by the then President Botha, as long as he *'unconditionally rejected violence as a political weapon'*, Mandela's response was:

'What freedom am I being offered while the organisation of the people [ANC] remains banned? Only free men can negotiate. A prisoner cannot enter into contracts.'

Mandela was completely sold on his vision of seeing apartheid abolished. It gave meaning to his suffering. He had a 'why' to live for and endured the suffering that came with it. In 1990, Mandela was released and went on to become the first black president of South Africa, a role he held from 1994 to 1998.

Use what's in your hands

You might be thinking there is no way you can accomplish anything on Mandela's scale. Well, firstly, says who? Whilst the likes of Mandela or even biblical heroes such as Apostle Paul and Joseph are no longer with us, the world still requires Bounce Back Heroes like them. As my Mum used to tell me when I came second or third in exams: *"Those ahead of you don't have two heads!'* The same goes for us today. Those heroic people are flesh and blood like you and me. What sets them apart is they used what was in their hands. That's what's going to set you apart. The world needs what's in your hands. Mandela said:

> 'It is in your hands to make of our world a better one for all.'

The items in your hands can include your experiences, a skill, gift or talent, as well as the essential Bounce Back attitudes and beliefs you may already possess. Combined and used wisely with the necessary support, you have what it takes.

Frankly speaking, I don't believe that all of those we read about in the Bible or the media who found meaning in and through their suffering started out knowing the great impact they would have on the world. Yet, their cumulative and seemingly small actions culminated in their world's being changed for the better. Some of those Bounce Back Heroes simply nurtured the vision and shared it with others, who, in turn, came on board and joined the cause.

It is worth bearing in mind that we all have a target audience for our vision and it is unlikely we are sent to reach everyone. For some, their audiences are large, while others' are small in number. The great news is that according to the parable of the talents in Matthew 25:14–30, it is not so much about the size of your talent, audience, or success (or lack thereof). What I believe God wants is that you use what you have been given. It is so liberating and comforting to know that as long as you and I invest our talents and experiences, instead of burying them, a reward awaits us.

In the moments when we feel like giving up, or the burden seems too much for us to bear, we have the help of the Holy Spirit who acts as our Counsellor, Helper, Intercessor, Advocate, Strengthener and Standby (John 14:16, AMP). We do not need to take this journey alone.

In closing, something I have done personally, to good effect, is creating a vision for my life. The ultimate goal that I work towards every day, which I have indelibly etched on my heart, is to hear my Lord say:

> *'Well done, good and faithful servant; you were faithful over a few things, I will make you ruler over many things. Enter into the joy of your lord.'*
> **(Matthew 25:21, NKJV)**

That's what I live for. And so when I cross over to the other side and make my way through the pearly gates, those are the words with which I want to greeted. Oh what joy! As for now, I continue to endure, with my purpose giving meaning to my life.

Arise and shine ... your purpose awaits!

Now we have looked at the concept of creating a meaning or purpose for your life experiences, the next step is to accept the challenge, realising you have what it takes to make it.

Accept your earthly mission

Accepting your mission is all about forging ahead with a view of bringing about positive change in your world. I am often inspired by the words of Isaiah 60:1–3. The Amplified version aptly puts it this way:

> 'Arise [from the depression and prostration in which circumstances have kept you—rise to a new life]! Shine (be radiant with the glory of the Lord), for your light has come, and the glory of the Lord has risen upon you!
> For behold, darkness shall cover the earth, and dense darkness [all] peoples, but the Lord shall arise upon you [O Jerusalem], and His glory shall be seen on you.
> And nations shall come to your light, and kings to the brightness of your rising."
> **(AMP)**

I love the way the scripture encourages us to rise up from the sadness and burdens our life experiences have tried to use to keep us down. I love it because it accepts that our life moments can indeed keep us down. Notwithstanding, the mandate is to rise to a new beginning. But the call is not only to rise up, but also to stand tall and take your place because God's glory is shining on you. So when you rise, you shine too. You reflect this glory to the extent that people, including people of power and influence, will be drawn to you. When we hide our innate light, no one gets to see it or benefit from it.

I have noticed that those who, despite their challenges, chose to rise, go on to attract the attention of others. I mentioned earlier that no matter where Joseph found himself, he always caught the attention of those around him, including Potiphar and Pharaoh. In the case of Esther, despite the Jews being in captivity, she rose to find the favour with king Ahasuerus. The same could be said of Daniel, who was also in captivity, yet his wisdom and ability to interpret dreams brought him before kings and brought about promotion. In more recent times, Nelson Mandela attracted a worldwide audience before, during and after his imprisonment. So you see, it is all about rising and taking our rightful place.

Every so often, when I come across an inspiring story I wonder what the impact would have been if the person hadn't managed to 'rise and shine'. What if Moses had not answered the call to deliver the Israelites? What impact would it have had on those in bondage? What if Esther had refused to approach the king boldly? What would have been the fate of the Jews of her time? What if David had been fearful of standing up to Goliath? What would have happened to the children of Israel? If Jesus had decided to remain in Heaven, as opposed to dying on the cross, how would we have been reconciled to God?

Take a look at the world around you today. Your life is benefiting from many others who arose, even in suffering. Someone, somewhere, fought so you can vote, have a voice, be educated, practice your faith, live healthier or even longer. Someone has suffered so you can live the way you do today. The way God used them in our yesterdays and yesteryears, to make a positive impact on our world today, is the same way He is looking for the likes of you and I to make a positive difference in other people's lives tomorrow. So, potentially, we are the modern day Josephs, Deborahs, Samuels, Elijahs, Pauls, etc.

In closing this section I leave you to ponder on a quote from Nelson Mandela:

> 'Our deepest fear is not that we are inadequate. Our deepest fear is that we are powerful beyond measure. It is our light, not our darkness, that most frightens us. We ask ourselves, Who am I to be brilliant, gorgeous, talented, fabulous? Actually, who are you not to be? You are a child of God. Your playing small does not serve the world. There is nothing enlightened about shrinking so that other people won't feel insecure around you. We are all meant to shine, as children do. We were born to make manifest the glory of God that is within us. It's not just in some of us; it's in everyone. And as we let our own light shine, we unconsciously give other people permission to do the same. As we are liberated from our own fear, our presence automatically liberates others.'

Coach Gee says:
We all need to rise up in our 'today' to ensure others benefit from our existence tomorrow. Doing otherwise, whilst chasing our own agenda, might be considered doing others an injustice.

You have been built to succeed

Every single one of us has the capability to bounce back. That ability lies buried within us. Pretty much the same way most new computers come preloaded with an operating system, we also come with the human equivalent. Our operating system is the Spirit of the living God, residing on the inside of us. This equips us to do what we are called to do, including developing resilience.

To get clarity of your capabilities, it is worth consulting your operating system manual, i.e. the Bible. This will give you an understanding of your Manufacturer (i.e. God) and see what support is available on His 'support' pages (i.e. the pages of the Bible). Using the analogy of a computer, below are some typical problems users (i.e. we) face along with biblical-based responses from your Manufacturer (God):

Problem: My system is running slow (procrastinating, feeling weary, overwhelmed).
Solution: If your machine is running slow, drop it off at our 24-hour care centre and we will boost its performance. Alternatively, you can connect with us remotely

but you will need to grant us access to your core so that we can root out the problem. Using our 24-hour chat facility, you can tell us the symptoms and upload all your worries. We can assure you peace of mind throughout the whole process (Manual reference: Isaiah 26:3; Matthew 11:28-30; John 14:27; 1 Peter 5:7).

Problem: I think my system has been hacked or invaded by a virus (I am facing attacks/opposition/adversity/suffering).
Solution: Your system was designed to resist every form of attack and was tested rigorously before release. To date, there are no known threats or attacks that can penetrate your inbuilt firewall to compromise your system or its performance. Moreover, each day you connect with the cloud, we fortify your system and stand on guard – protecting your system. And even if there was the possibility of attack, you need do nothing. If they come close to your firewall, they self-destruct! (Manual reference: Psalm 68:19; Isaiah 54:17; 2 Chronicles 20).

Problem: I cannot find my make and model info (I have lost my identity, lost track of my worth)
Solution: You are our masterpiece! Designed by hand and wonderfully fashioned. There is none other like you, nor would there ever be. You have been set apart from all other models – the Manufacturer's very own premium range (Genesis 1:26; Psalm 138:8; Psalm 139:14; 1 Peter 2:9).

Problem: My system is outdated/needs an upgrade (feeling ineffective, out of touch, left behind, powerless and empty).
Solution: We offer free lifetime upgrades and check-ups. It is all free and part of the service: our lifetime commitment to you. Keep an eye on your inbuilt core performance indicator though. It will tell you when you need to check in. PS: Never override the warning signs. (Manual reference: Zechariah 4:6-7; Matthew 11:28–30; John 4:1–26).

Problem: Software missing (I feel incapable).
Solution: You have a lifetime, all-inclusive service with us. Simply identify what you need and download it from the Manufacturer's cloud. (Manual reference: Philippians 4:13 and 19)

Problem: System failure/crash (Feel stuck after a difficult time, lost sense of purpose /vision)
Solution: In the rare event that your system crashes and seems to die on you, just say the special code 'L.I.V.E.' into the external microphone and it should power up in less than ten seconds. (Manual reference: Ezekiel 37 and Psalm 118:17).

* * *

So now the ball is in your court. You need to make a decision as to whether you accept the call on your life. The reality is you are here, in the present and in this moment, for such a time as this. Moreover, you have already been equipped to do the job. Will you accept the challenge? I leave you with this quote from Dr Munroe's book, *Understanding Your Potential:*

> 'You must decide if you are going to rob the world or bless it with the rich, valuable, potent, untapped resources locked away within you.'

Coach Gee says:

My prayer is that you will come to a place of fully embracing the potential and greatness that lies within you. So if you still think you are disqualified, for one reason or another, think twice. You have the innate ability to fulfil your life call. It's not about strength or power. It is about having a passion to see the vision fulfilled.

Become unstoppable

This is where the fun part begins. The aim is to get you mobilised by stoking the fires of your heart. I remember an experiment we did in science class using smoke particles. In normal room temperature, the smoke particles were barely moving. However, when the temperature was increased, the smoke particles started to vibrate and eventually began to bounce off the walls. My hope is that as we make our way through this section, you will be (re)energised by your passions.

Step out of the boat (you won't drown!)

Has there ever been a time you really wanted to do something and you were about to take the plunge when, all of a sudden, you were paralysed with fear? And you backed off? Perhaps you became anxious about the 101 things that could go wrong? Maybe you listened to those I call *dream killers* and naysayers who left you feeling deflated and a failure even before you started? And, as a consequence, all you saw was 'doom and gloom' and you never got beyond the starting line.

Sadly, this is where many people get stuck. But the reality is if you want to step out, you really need to do it in faith. And to walk on water requires one simple thing: stepping out of the boat! There is no other way around it.

Over the years I have come across people who seem to be waiting for some sort of miraculous sign or divine intervention, like the parting of the Red sea or money raining down from heaven. Some have put out fleeces, looked for handwriting on the wall, waited to be called out of a crowd, and so on. Whilst God is able to do all that, He does not always operate that way. Instead, what I have seen Him do, time and time again, is take the little that you have and multiply it. So that when you take a step towards Him to do all that He has called you to do, He has something to work with. Taking that small step builds your confidence too.

Let me give you an example. As an author and speaker, I hear a shedload of women say they want to write a book. They go on to share how they feel God wants them to use their story to encourage other women. 'Great!' I say, and then ask them what they have done about it. Their response is invariably disheartening for me because 9.9 out of 10 are yet to put pen to paper. I wish I had collected £1 or even £0.01p from each of them, because I would be loaded right now.

I appreciate that some people don't know where to start and that can be daunting, but the sure way to eat an elephant is to take a bite at a time. There are books, courses and other resources, yet many simply fail to step out of the boat. And, of course, there is our trusted friend 'Google'. I have been known to type in questions and get the answers I need.

Anyway, helping women embark on these journeys inspired by their feeling of purpose was one of the reasons I started my academy. In an effort to awaken the writer in them, I say, *'Perhaps start with writing your idea and then commit to jotting down your thoughts daily'*. For those who seem more keen, they often manage to grab a mini-coaching session from me where I share my experiences. Again, they get excited, but it is usually short-lived. Years later, when our paths cross again, their evasive expressions answer the burning question within me: *'So where is the book?'* And so for many, writing the book they felt they were born to write simply becomes a fantasy, as opposed to something they see as paramount to their calling. To me, that is a real shame and a 'waste of their pain'.

So what happens when the writer fails to write? Nothing! And what could happen if you start to write? The possibilities are endless. I should know. I remember when I really felt the nudge to do so after accepting redundancy from my job. I knew I had to write but I gave God excuses as to how I did not have a writing contract or how I needed to make money to live on. So I focused on building my business and never gave myself the time to do it.

Anyway, after a frustrating few months of things not going my way, I hit a brick wall. And I ended up having a spiritual fit and holy tantrum. Out of frustration I said to God, *'What do You want from me?'* His answer was simple: *'Write the book!'* And so I did.

I wrote morning, noon and night. I wrote between four and eight hours a day, and I kept this up for many months (PS: Now I have been writing for years I can write a lot faster ☺). Anyway, the manuscript was done and I breathed a sigh of relief, thinking, like a child: *'Finished. Look what I have done'*. If the truth be told, I was unsure what was going to happen. This was back in the day when the only way to get published was if, by miracle, your book was fished out of a 'slush pile' and considered commercial enough to be published, and that could take years, if not forever. Not knowing what was next, I kind of twiddled my thumbs, expecting something great to happen. And it did.

I met a wonderful lady, who happened to be one of the guest speakers at my church's annual women's conference. She was an author with a number of books under her belt and I was in awe. We struck up a conversation as I was driving her back to her hotel. And to cut a long story short, she introduced me to her publisher in the USA (NB: That's another route to getting published). And that's how my first two books were published – *Overcoming Negative Emotions* and *Overcoming Emotional Baggage*. How did it happen? We simply got into a conversation and I mentioned I had just completed my manuscript. If I'd said I had a book I wanted to write, I doubt I would have gotten that once-in-a-lifetime opportunity.

From that experience, I came to learn a valuable lesson: when we think we are waiting for God, He, in turn, is waiting for us to take the first step. I also believe that success comes from preparation meeting opportunity. Even the Bible says be ready in season and out of season. You just never know when that time of favour or that divine connection will take place.

Remember the time Peter saw Jesus walking on the water in Matthew 14:22–26? He asked Jesus to allow him to walk on the water too. Jesus responded by saying, '*Come*'. Do you think Jesus was ignorant of the fact that He had just asked Peter to step out of a boat and into the sea (a turbulent one at that)? Regardless, Jesus still said, '*Come*'. Now Peter could have said, '*I'll come only if You part the sea for me*', or '*Send angels to carry me over the water*', or even '*No Lord, You come and get me!*'. Rather, he obeyed in faith and stepped out of the boat, contrary to what his head may have been saying to him. So Peter put some action to his faith just like James 2:17 encourages us to.

Until you step out, you will <u>never</u> have your 'Peter experience' nor will you know what God could have done with your simple faith and obedience. By the way, what do you think would happen if you were to step out of your boat? Do you think God is going to let you drown? That's not in His nature. As long as you remain close to Him and trust Him, all will be well. Going back to Peter's story, Jesus' hands were already there to grab Peter's hands.

Coach Gee says:
If you are still in doubt about stepping out, maybe you need to reflect on how much you trust God. Unlike people who may say one thing and do another, God is NOT like that. The Bible tells us that His Word is worthy of our trust (Psalm 33:4). If He says it, He will do it. He is like none other. So maybe your prayer should be, *'Lord, teach me to trust You so I can step out of the boat when I need to'*.

Let your passion fuel your purpose

Your passion for your purpose is what will fuel you to do what might seem ridiculous to others. That's what happened to Legson Kayira. At the tender age of sixteen, he had a seemingly impossible dream, which was to get a degree in the USA. The only challenge was he had no means of getting there. But that did not stop this Bounce Back Hero! He started his epic journey from a small rural Malawian village – walking barefoot. All he had for the journey was five days' worth of food, an axe and two books – *Pilgrim's Progress* and the Bible.

Kayira travelled more than 2,500 miles across four African countries. Eventually he reached Sudan where the American consulate supported him by offering travel to the USA so he could take up a scholarship at Skagit Valley College in Washington State. Kayira later went to study History at the University of Cambridge and was the author of a number of books. In his book, *I Will Try*, a New York Times Bestseller, he wrote:

> '*I learned I was not, as most Africans believed, the victim of my circumstances but the master of them.*'

When I first read about Kayira, I thought, OMG! How does a young lad of sixteen make such a seemingly impossible mission a reality? The answer is one step at a time – literally, in his case. With each step, moving out into the unknown world of foreign people, dialects, cultures and potential dangers, he saw himself realising his dream. His present circumstances or afflictions did not hold him back. Rather, his mission gave him the passion, determination, courage and hope to keep going. According to Friedrich Nietzsche, Kayira found his 'why' to live for, and, as a result, he was willing to bear any 'how' to make it happen.

What a wonderfully inspiring story this is, and it goes to show, according to Don Ward: '*If your dream is big enough, the facts don't count*'. You might be thinking, '*Yeah right. You don't know my story*'. That may be true but I also know that people can do just about anything they set their minds to. Even our heavenly Father noted this when the people of Babel got together, in unity, with a mission to build a tower that reached the skies (Genesis 11:1–9).

He recognised that people could do whatever they set their hearts on. That should not be surprising, though, as we are made in the image of God.

However, the point to note here is that while the story focused on unity in a group of people, the same principle applies to individuals. If you are not 'united' within yourself, that what you set out to do can be achieved, failure will be imminent. You need to be completely sold on your dream/vision or you may abandon it when the going gets tough. And the fact is, tough times will come! Everyone who has achieved any level of success has faced them along the way. Furthermore, if you don't buy into your own dream or vision one hundred per cent, it is unlikely others will.

So, first things first, you need to be clear on what you should be doing. Next, it's about passionately pursuing it in an unstoppable fashion. Also, it pays to always remember that you are never alone on this exciting journey. God is right there with you; there to offer you assistance. Like Jesus did whilst here on Earth, who recognised He could not do anything apart from God. So He prayed. Adopting this approach will give you the confidence to forge ahead. I believe Isaiah 50:7 puts it beautifully:

'And the Master, God, stays right there and helps me, so I'm not disgraced. Therefore I set my face like flint, confident that I'll never regret this.'
(MSG)

Coach Gee says:
Let this be your strategy: set your face like a flint and go for it.

Reflective Questions

- Keeping in mind the combination of skills, talents and challenging life experiences you possess: how can you put them to great(er) use – to better your 'world'?
- Do you have a vision for your life? If not, create one and write the vision down (Habakkuk 2:2). Make it something compelling enough that it gets you out of bed in the morning.
- Think about our world today: What if farmers stopped growing food and singers/musicians refused to perform? What if teachers refused to teach; writers stopped writing? What if leaders did not lead and preachers refused to preach? What impact would this have on our world? Now, let's bring it closer to home: what is the world missing today because you are not living purposefully? What impact is that having on someone's life today? Could a person's wellbeing, safety, growth, salvation, healing, confidence, encouragement, success, or even life be reliant on you taking your rightful place? No pressure but worth considering.

Chapter Nine

Now, Pay It Forward!

Over the previous chapters, my goal has been to change your perspectives on your challenging life experiences with a view to turn the experience into something positive. This chapter is all about putting what you have read into practice. However, before we dive in I want to share a little bit about how the Pay It Forward concept came about.

The notion was based on the American movie called *Pay It Forward*. In the movie, a school teacher (Kevin Spacey) gives his class an assignment to come up with a plan that would change the world for better. One of his students (Hayley Joel Osment) comes up with a charitable programme based on a network of good deeds, which he calls *Pay It Forward*. The whole idea was that when someone received a favour, that person was to pay it back (or forward, as it were) to three other people. The caveat is that the favour cannot be something the recipient can do for themselves.

The result makes an inspirational movie to watch. I would recommend it.

So I am now asking you to come up with a mission or project of your own to help others. You are not bound to three people and you can make it as big or small as your imagination and guts will allow you. Key to this is either creating a project around your challenging experiences (e.g. to help others in a similar situation) OR finding some way of using your experience to propel you into committing yourself to your life purpose or other worthy cause. Of course, it could be that both of these are one and the same. Either way, your project needs to make a positive impact in your world. And in choosing to do it, you are electing to bounce back and make something good out of your adversity or challenge. You are laughing in the face of the situation and saying, *'You can't keep me down! I am rising and shining. I am a star that cannot be quenched'*.

To help you along, the remainder of this chapter aims to give you some help in starting your journey as a Bounce Back Hero and embarking on your Pay It Forward project. But, before we dive in, below you will find a recap of what we have covered, which I am calling the Ten Principles of Bouncing Back.

The Ten Principles of Bouncing Back

Principle one: Life happens. And when it does, it can seem unfair. But flip adversity/suffering on its head and choose to bounce back.

Principle two: Whatever happens, God is still in control and He has a plan for you. So trust Him.

Principle three: Just because you get knocked down by life does not mean you have to stay down. Rather, do whatever it takes to get back in the saddle. Arise and shine.

Principle four: Maximise your downtime. Use the opportunity to work on yourself.

Principle five: Adopt a Bounce Back Hero mindset by changing your perspectives and becoming adaptable.

Principle six: Hope keeps us alive, no matter what we face. It gives us a 'why' to live, meaning we can bear any 'how'.

Principle seven: Maximise your waiting-room experience. You may not get that time again.

Principle eight: Create a meaning for your life, even when your life seems to be shattered like a broken ornament. Rather than going back to your old life, piece together the broken pieces and make something new.

Principle nine: When you fully accept your personal mission on earth, you become enabled to press on, even in dark moments.

Principle ten: Let your passion fuel your personal mission. Choose to become unstoppable.

Keep these at the back of your mind at all times and remind yourself of them.

Have a clear mission

I am hoping that as you have been working your way through this book you have had some time to prayerfully think about your life mission or purpose. I am of the belief that your mission is strongly connected to your life experiences and/or the special skills and talents you possess. In any case, both assist each other.

Perhaps you have always been passionate about something or the passion has come as a result of your experiences? Maybe you have an innate ability to do something others struggle with? Perhaps there is an issue (e.g. in your life, church, workplace, local school or community, etc.) that ignites your emotions or a response (e.g. makes you angry or take action); or when it comes up, you feel you can no longer stand by, watch and do nothing.

All these (and more) are tell-tale signs of your mission. Where some people get stuck is in not knowing exactly what they should be doing. When I face such moments, including times of adversity, I adopt my two-pronged approach, which I mentioned before. Firstly, I seek Father, as He has the blueprints to my life. He knows why I am here. And seeing none of us is a 'mistake', it makes sense to start with Him. Secondly, In addition to my life experiences, I am also looking at what's in my hands, i.e. what gifts I have been blessed with. Father must have thought, '*I need a Gladys to write some books for Me. So I will send her at such and such a time and give her some gifts to help her along*'. He not only gave me what I needed to achieve it but He also put the desire in me to write. Over the years this 'raw' gift has been shaped, refined and sharpened. The result is that my writing skills have improved with time (so my editor, Wanda, tells me). The more you use what you have been blessed with, the better you get at it. Furthermore, you become more confident in your abilities and begin to appreciate them more.

Let me use myself as an example. With regard to emotional baggage, I knew God wanted me to do something about this after my personal experiences and the women I was meeting. Moreover, I was frustrated by the fact that there didn't seem to be any support available at the time. So the nudge came to write about the challenges women faced whilst offering practical, biblical-based, simple solutions women could apply. That's how *Overcoming Negative Emotions* and *Overcoming Emotional Baggage* came about.

But it did not stop there, and it became evident that God had a plan. The publication of the books created new opportunities such as speaking engagements in the church and beyond, meaning my reach expanded to new audiences. But it did not end there. As I became increasingly associated with the topic, many women started approaching me for help. Some turned to me because they wanted to tell their story whilst others came because they felt there wasn't any support in their churches. Over time, I felt another fatherly nudge that was to have me launch annual conferences. This was later followed by an annual retreat.

Can you see how one experience has grown into something that has now had a positive impact on thousands of women? God has a knack of using every bit of our lives for His glory. This includes the things to which you don't give a second thought, such as your values, strengths, weaknesses, qualities, gifts, likes, dislikes, etc. So don't discount any aspect of your life, including your challenging moments. It all forms part of the picture. Let me break this down for you and show you how God can use even snippets of our lives. I will use myself again as an example. This is a snapshot of myself in relation to my Overcoming Emotional Baggage mission:

Experience:
- Carrying/struggling with emotional baggage.
- Finding little or no support within the church/Christian domain.
- Meeting other women facing similar experiences.
- Writing column articles for women's magazines (I did this for a number of years)

Passions:
- Empowering women and giving them the confidence to chase their dreams.
- Creating resources to meet the needs of women as a women's wealth and success coach.

Gifts:
- Writing
- Encouraging/inspiring others
- Being innovative and resourceful
- Leading others
- Being a pioneer

Skills:
- Coaching
- Speaking
- Training/developing others
- Writing
- Organising/planning
- Attention to detail

Personality traits
- Go-getter
- Dreamer
- Introvert

Strengths
- Determination
- Willingness to take action
- Focused
- Perseverance
- Resilience, bouncing back no matter what

Dislikes
- Women suffering
- Injustice

My Overcoming Emotional Baggage mission came about by using a combination of the afore mentioned, depending on the task I was being asked to do, e.g. writing, speaking, creating products, running a conference or retreat.

So over to you. I would like you to think about your mission by considering what you bring to the table. Doing this will give you a clearer understanding of who you are as a person and bring clarity as to the mission you are charged with. Unless you take the time to do this you may well end up chasing a mission that is, quite frankly, someone else's. Before you dive in, remember to invite Father into the situation.

Action: Uncovering your mission

1. **Uncover what you bring to the table:** Using the Notes section at the back of this book, or any other note-taking device, make a list of what you consider to be your key experiences (including your challenging life situations), passion, gifts, skills, personality traits, strengths, and dislikes.
   Coaching Tip: Notice that I intentionally did not include achievements, qualifications, etc., as I don't want you to get side-tracked by these. Whilst they can help, the secret to success does not necessarily rely on them.

2. **Identify your mission:** From your list, can you identify what might be your mission? Prayerfully consider this and make notes. Is there a project now staring you in

the face? Can you see the beginnings of a life mission? Is it something you are meant to be doing – fulltime or part-time? Pray about it.

Coaching Tip: Just in case you are worrying how it can all come together to make something purposeful and profitable, relax! Many others share this concern too (including me). Don't worry about it. Your aim is to discover the heart of Father on the matter and launch out. My advice is to be faithful in all that you do and God will do the rest. By the way, did you notice how I never got the instruction to do a conference first? I probably would have fainted! It all started with writing (articles and books), and, over time, God built on this. So, obedience is the key.

3. **Identify who your target audience is:** And before you say that word most people fall into the trap of saying – 'EVERYONE', ask Father to show you to whom you are to reach out. We all have a target audience we are to reach, and it is likely your experience will point to this, though it is still worth asking.

   Coaching Tip: It may be that you have a primary audience, which may or may not be expanded later to a secondary audience. Either way, don't fall into the trap of trying to save the whole world, as you will end up saving no one at all. It may be tempting, but stick with your mission! From time to time men ask me when there will be an *Overcoming Emotional Baggage for Men* book or conference. As exciting as it sounds, I am yet to get the heavenly nudge to launch this.

Plus, it's not a major passion of mine (sorry guys) nor is it my primary call. So, that idea stays on the shelf for now. Plus, I've got other stuff to keep me going for at least two lifetimes!

4. **Make a list of the goals and tasks you are to accomplish:** These are specific actions you will need to take to help you achieve your goal, and ultimately your mission. What do you feel Father is nudging you to do? Make a note of these things.
Coaching Tip: By the way, your tasks can include things you are to do, as well as those you are NOT to do. For instance, when I was asked to write the book I was also told to quit my role as a columnist. In my years of working with God I have often found that in order for me to receive something new (often bigger and better) I often needed to let go of what I was holding on to – as precious as it may have been to me. Sometimes, you have to slam shut a door behind you before the one in front of you opens.

By the end of this exercise, you should have a clearer picture of your mission and the outline of what needs to be done. Take your time and prayerfully consider these.

Make it happen

I came across an awesome quote from the late Dr Myles Munroe, which states:

'The poorest man in the world is the man without a dream. The most frustrated man in the world is the man with a dream that never becomes reality.'

In order for us to make our dream or mission a reality, action is necessary. Without this, they simply become a wish list and never see the light of day. Moreover, you will become frustrated. So, now is the time to make them a reality.

S.M.A.R.T.-proof your goals

Your mission will need to be broken down into goals. And any goal that you hope to accomplish must pass the S.M.A.R.T. test, adapted from George T. Doran's 1981 article, *'There's a S.M.A.R.T. way to write management's goals and objectives'*.

Your goals ought to be,

Specific, Measurable, Achievable, Realistic/Relevant and Time-bound

Without this, it is unlikely you will get far with your mission.

Action: S.M.A.R.T.-proofing your goals

1. Using the S.M.A.R.T. test, go through each of your listed goals and ensure it fulfils the S.M.A.R.T. test criteria. Consider the following:

    Specific
    Is it clear, unambiguous, well-defined? Think of the what, when, why, how, where, who.

    Measurable
    What are the criteria for measuring progress? How can you tell if it's been achieved?

    Achievable
    This needs to be just out of your reach but doable.

    Realistic/Relevant
    You need to be willing and able to do this. It also needs to be relevant to your purpose.

    Time-bound
    Do you have enough time to achieve it? When do you plan to achieve it?

2. Re-evaluate and/or put aside any goals that do not pass the test.

Create your action plan

The aim of your action plan is to break your goal(s) into specific actions and associate reasonable deadlines for each one. Break these down into 'bite-size' chunks. You may also need to do some research into your goal and ensure all the necessary steps are accounted for. Furthermore, I suggest you prioritise your actions, as some may be more important than others, especially those time-critical actions. Also, don't forget to build in contingencies.

One point to note is that whilst I am all for dedication and putting your all into your goals, don't make the mistake of making your action plan a noose around your neck. There is nothing worse than buckling under the insurmountable pressure you put on yourself, unless there is a reason for it (periodically, such a need might arise, but not all the time). This is a trap any of us can fall into, especially when we are so passionate about our mission. If care is not taken, you could find yourself either stressed or burnt out, quitting or resenting your mission.

Manage your mission goals

Now this is the point at which many fail, simply because their goals are not managed well – if at all. All goals have to be managed so as not to jeopardise your mission. Just like a plant, your goals need to be fed, watered and nurtured or else they will die!

Once you have created your goals, I suggest you place them in a visible place. The last thing you want is to hide them away somewhere where they gather dust – the physical or virtual kind. So why not print it out and place where you can see it. The fridge door works wonders, so does your bathroom mirror or anywhere you use regularly.

Also, part of managing your goals requires you to review your progress. I suggest you do this periodically, in line with your deadlines. I tend to set alerts in my electronic calendar that prompts me. That way I can keep abreast of how I am getting on.

The reason you need to manage your goals is that life has a habit of getting in the way. Regardless of whether your mission is your fulltime job or not, you still have other aspects of your life to factor in such as relationships, job/career (if applicable), home and church life (and all that comes with it), your other roles and responsibilities and the like. Therefore, your objective is to manage all the other areas of your life so that they do not suffer nor does your mission get kicked to the curb.

Get the support and resources you need

On your journey to fulfilling your mission, you will need a whole load of resources to make them a reality. The following are my top two:

Create your M.I.S.S.I.O.N. team

People are our greatest asset and we all need people in our corner in their various capacities. Your M.I.S.S.I.O.N. team consists of the following:

M is for Mentors

These are people you look up to who can offer you advice and wisdom based on their experience and areas of expertise. Your mentors would typically be operating at the level you are aspiring to reach, and your goal is to learn from them. In doing so, you slash your learning time immensely. Plus, you don't have to waste time or money making the same mistakes they made in their early days. So, prayerfully seek people who can support you – even if it means paying for their time. Trust me, it is worth it! By the way, virtual mentors, i.e. people to whom you have no physical access, can be equally powerful, as you can learn by observing them, reading their resources, attending their events, etc. I often seek out people who are doing what I want to be doing and see if there is anything to learn, including what I should and should not do. There is always something to learn!

I is for Influencers
These are people who are well-connected in the field you are trying to penetrate. They are seen to be in the know, and are influential. With your influencer, what they know (their opinion) and who they know (their large networks) count. They can help boost interest in your mission. These individuals can include marketing/public relation professionals, bloggers, journalists, people in certain roles, e.g. influential church/Christian leaders, and the like. Before you reach out, do some research on them (their audience, sphere of influence, and reputation). Also, be clear about what you want out of the relationship and what you want them to influence. I would suggest you approach them when you have your mission product, service or brand in place.

S is for Supporters

Supporters are your encouragers, your fan base, who are passionate about what you do and/or what you stand for. They are the ones who will wholeheartedly encourage you along the journey. They do so in many ways through their words, time, money, and much more. I have benefitted from these as they have come at crucial moments in my mission. I do believe God always raises supporters to keep us going. It is worth noting that your supporters might well include people who embrace your vision with much charisma and energy in the first stage, then float away when they lose interest. These people are useful energisers and we all need them. However, what you should look out for are supporters who will be the 'troopers' you can rely on.

S is for Success Coach

Whilst you may have the passion and talent, you still need a coach to help you reach your goals. Ever wondered why athletes, sports teams, or business executives have coaches? To help them reach their goals. Working with a coach means you get the support in creating a strategy and a robust action plan. They keep you focused and motivated whilst helping you modify your attitudes, beliefs and behaviours to cultivate success. They 'push' more than you are likely to push yourself, meaning success is more likely than if you were struggling on your own. This is a worthy investment for those who are serious-minded. I have used coaches throughout my career to help with various goals.

I is for Intercessor

In short, an intercessor is someone who intervenes on your behalf in prayer. Not everyone is blessed with this gift, but for those who are, it is their call. The fact is you have dared to arise and shine. However, equally, there will be opposing forces intent on keeping you down. So, in addition to your own prayers (you don't abdicate this responsibility to the intercessor), ask intercessors to keep you and your mission in prayer. Trust me when I say your survival and success depends on this. I have a network of people praying for me. This includes my ministry team, my mother (the greatest intercessor I know) and a few other close confidantes. To help your intercessors pray effectively, periodically give them specific prayer points and/or when you need specific help (e.g. when you need to make key decisions, when you/the mission is under attack, etc.). As trust is a basis for this relationship, choose wisely.

O is for Operators

Depending on your project size, you may need one or more people to help you achieve your goals. They can help with the tasks you cannot do, do not want to do or perhaps should not be doing (PS: if you refuse to let go, you may lose focus and perhaps limit the effectiveness of your mission). Your operators can include volunteers, interns, assistants, managers, third-party suppliers or partners.

And if you wonder whether you are cut out to lead a project yourself, perhaps you'll choose to be a team-player. You might join a local initiative to help children read in a local primary school or join a team of other volunteers to cook at weekends for a soup kitchen, for example. With your help the mission is realised, and it helps you achieve your goals too. Over time, you may find yourself in the roles of both leader and team-player.

N is for Network
By this, I mean your own personal network of peers, associates, colleagues, friends, family and much more. Never forget the power of your network. I am of the opinion that all you need is within your reach – either directly, through these individuals, or indirectly, through their own networks. Within your personal network, identify those who can become your Bounce Back Buddies, who are perhaps embarking upon missions of their own. As buddies, you can offer each other valuable moral support. You can bounce ideas off each other and perhaps pool resources, if applicable.

* * *

Whatever you do, plan to have your M.I.S.S.I.O.N. team in place. This is not something to skip over. Furthermore, it is worth doing research on who is to form part of this team. Whilst at it, don't discount those in your network. Your M.I.S.S.I.O.N. team may be closer than you think.

One important note to keep in mind is to avoid being unequally yoked in your relationships. Don't partner/hook up with someone who does not 'get' you and/or where you are right now. There have been times I have tried to explain to others what I am trying to do and all I get back is a blank stare or they try to shoot the idea down with negative words even before it gets a chance. So I suggest keeping away naysayers/pessimists, people who are stuck and are not willing to do what it takes to become unstuck (the best you could do for them is give them a copy of this book and keep them in your prayers); or those on a completely different journey to you (e.g. who need emotional/spiritual restoration). In doing this, you avoid the baggage that comes along with such. Accept that not everyone can go with you to your next level. This is a painful truth I have had to embrace.

Action: Build your M.I.S.S.I.O.N team

Take some time to prayerfully identify individuals who can become part of your M.I.S.S.I.O.N team. Also note that, over time, some of these will change, as not everyone will be in for the long haul.

Financial support

When I say money, I mean something you can exchange for what you need/want. In our world today, currency is what is used to trade. If you need a computer or laptop to start writing your books, you need money to buy one. Even if you decide to start small with a pen and notebook, these still need to be purchased.

Without the necessary funding to support you, the mission, just like any project, can be starved to extinction.

That said, I don't believe you need to have millions in your pocket to start either. So, I say consider the following:

Use what's in your hands: What do you have in your hands that can earn you some income? We <u>all</u> have something in our hands we can exchange for money. Some of the Jesus' disciples were fishermen. Apostle Paul was a tent maker. So, I ask you to consider what's in your hands.

Surround yourself with the right people: Another key point to consider is that having the right people around you may prove more financially beneficial to you that money itself. With the right people around you in life, you can bounce back from wherever you find yourself (e.g. debt, business failure, etc.). Within the context of fulfilling your mission, God may have people already lined up to fund the project. I believe this was the case with our Lord Jesus Christ. During His three-year ministry, He did not work as a carpenter (He quit carpentry the moment His ministry began). Yet people who bought into the vision of His mission surrounded him, and they demonstrated their loyalty to it by either becoming co-labourers (i.e. operators), or by funding His ministry. The latter was necessary, as even Jesus had taxes to pay!

* * *

In closing, I am convinced from the precedent the Bible sets out that God <u>always</u> makes provision for the vision. Whilst He may not plant a money tree in your backyard, you have something to exchange for what you need – whether it be through you or others. So ask Father to open your spiritual eyes to see what He sees. Has He placed kingdom treasurers in your life to support you? Are there people willing to roll up their sleeves and join you? Perhaps it is time to let them in once you have prayerfully identified them.

Conclusion

Finishing Well

Survive! Thrive!! Maximise!!!

> *'The greatest tragedy in life is not death, but a life without a purpose.'*
> **Dr Myles Munroe**

We have come to the end of the journey, though I have a sneaky suspicion that this is just the beginning of a new journey for you. You are now tasked with using what you have learnt to survive, thrive and maximise whatever you have faced. Make all the 'hell' you have been through count for something! Refuse to let life keep you down, and fight back. Better still, bounce back and start living purposefully.

Spread your wings and fly

> *'Your existence is evidence that this generation needs something that your life contains.'*
>
> **Dr Myles Munroe**

Granted, life happened, but you don't have to become dysfunctional as a result of it, nor does it have to rob you of your purpose. The fact that you are here tells me that you have something of value to offer. So grab back the reins of your life, tap into your inner power, and soar above your circumstances. It is worth remembering that you have been designed to bounce back. You have been built to succeed. So, spread your wings and fly. Do us all proud and leave your mark on this earth.

You are not alone

In the moments when the journey seems daunting or you want to give up, always remember you are never alone. God has your back! In His divine wisdom He has orchestrated all the resources you will need to make it. Furthermore, there is an army of Bounce Back Heroes who have gone ahead of you, who are cheering you on. Here is what some are saying to you:

Paul is telling you to not faint or get weary of doing good (Galatians 6: 9).
David says you should encourage yourself in the Lord (I Samuel 30: 6).
Nehemiah reminds you of the fact that the Joy of the Lord is your strength (Nehemiah 8: 10).
Esther affirms you that you are born for such a time as this (Esther 4: 14).
Joseph says that God will turn every evil plan for your good (Genesis 50: 20).
Elisha is making you aware that things will be different this time tomorrow (2 Kings 7: 1).
The Shunammite woman holds up a placard with 'It is well' written on it (2 Kings 4).
When you feel overwhelmed, Jeremiah reminds you that nothing is impossible with God because nothing is too hard for Him (Jeremiah 32: 17).
And when you stumble and fall, Jesus will say, 'Talitha, cumi,' which means, 'Little girl, I say to you, arise.' (Mark 5: 41).

(Modified excerpt from *Healing a Discouraged Heart*)

So you go for it.

And lastly, today, I award you Bounce Back Hero-in-the-making status. Take courage and let your light shine for all to see. I am cheering you all the way. See you at the finish line.

Take the Bounce Back Pledge

To show you are serious about bouncing back and making your pain count for something, take the bounce back pledge below. By the way, if you would like to download a copy or share with others, visit www.gladysfministries.com

* * *

The Bounce Back Pledge

I, _____ (insert your name) solemnly promise to never waste my pain. Instead, I will do all that I can, in Gods strength and with the support of others, to overcome whatever hand life has dealt me and turn my pain into something positive.

I accept that life happens. And when it does, I choose to flip the adversity/suffering/challenge on its head. I choose to bounce back, regardless.

Whatever happens, I recognise that God is still in control of my life and He has a plan for me. Because of this, I choose to trust Him no matter what.

Whilst life may knock me down, I refuse to stay down. With God's help, I will get back in the saddle again, for I can do all things through Christ Jesus who strengthens me. I will rise and shine because God's glory is shining over me.

I choose to maximise my downtime. During such times, I will use the opportunity to work on myself, so I come back better and not bitter. I promise to listen out for any lessons my life is trying to bring to my attention.

I promised to always adopt a Bounce Back Hero mindset by changing my perspectives and becoming adaptable. I choose to renew my mind and feed it with wholesome, nurturing and uplifting content.

I will endeavour to always keep hope alive, no matter what I face. Because I have a 'why' to live, I will gain the strength to bear any 'how'. I am no longer fearful of my future. Rather, I am hopeful and excited.

I will always maximise my waiting-room experience and use my time wisely. As a result, I will emerge stronger, wiser, more mature, restored and replenished.

I choose to create a meaning for my life, even when I may struggle to piece together the pieces of my life. Rather than trying to make things like they were, I choose to seek out new opportunities to transform the course of my life.

I fully accept and embrace my personal mission here on earth. I will create a vision for the future and use whatever is in my hands to serve others. I will also build my M.I.S.S.I.O.N. team around me to help me fulfil my mission/purpose.

I choose to let my passion fuel my personal mission.

I will always step out of the boat in faith, refusing to be held down by fear. From today onwards, I become unstoppable.

So help me God!

Name: Date:

Signature:

Discover More Bounce Back! Resources

We recognise that this is the beginning of the journey for many readers. And so we are already working on a number of other ways to support you – the next generation of Bounce Back Heroes. So why not join our network and we will keep you posted on further services and products. To find out more or be kept updated, visit www.gladysfministries.com.

Here is what we have lined up for you:

Bounce Back! For Businesses/Organisations: Offering consulting, coaching, training and speaking services to organisations.

Bounce Back! Live: Offering seminars and workshops with Gladys Famoriyo.

Bounce Back! Mastermind Groups: Involving peer-to-peer mentoring, brainstorming, accountability and support, in a group setting, to support group members achieve success with their Pay It Forward projects.

Bounce Back! for Small Groups: Resources for group facilitators and individuals in small groups.

Bounce Back Hero! Book: This will be a collection of stories about ordinary people who have bounced back and made a positive difference in their worlds. If you want to be featured in this book, let us know. Send an email to bounceback@gladysfministries.com and tell us why.

Audios & Videos: Aimed at supporting you further and keeping you inspired.

Follow us | Like us | Engage with us
Facebook/GladysFamoriyoMinistries
Twitter: @GladysFMinistry | #bounceback4good
Youtube.com/GladysFamoriyoMinistriesInternational

Start Paying It Forward Today!

Help Someone Bounce Back!
With Compassion UK by Sponsoring a Child

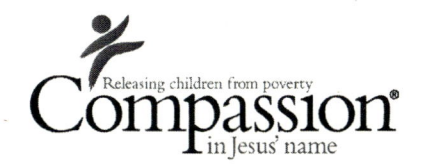

Compassion
Releasing children from poverty
in Jesus' name

YOU CAN CHANGE THE STORY — MY SPONSOR CHANGED MY LIFE

Compassion is an international Christian child development and child advocacy ministry. Partnering with local churches, it is committed to the spiritual, economic, social and physical development of children living in extreme poverty in 26 countries, enabling them to become responsible, fulfilled Christian adults.

If you want to make a positive difference in someone's life, you can start by sponsoring a child.

Find out more by visiting www.compassionuk.org. Be sure to mention Gladys Famoriyo Ministries and the *Bounce Back!* book.

About The Author

Gladys Famoriyo is an award-winning and best-selling author who speaks internationally. She has been in the transformational industry for over 19 years and remains passionate about empowering people, especially women, so they live purposefully, maximising their wealth of experiences, talents and skills, whilst making a positive difference in their worlds. In March 2015, she was awarded the Inspirational Woman Award by Wise Women Awards for her efforts in this field.

Gladys is a prolific writer. Her books include *Overcoming Emotional Baggage: A Woman's Guide to Living the Abundant Life* (0-924748-73-7), *Healing a Discouraged Heart: Getting Back on Track When Life Lets You Down* (978-0-9562606-3-5) and *Quit Hiding, Start Living! How Women Can Free Themselves From Past Hurts* (978-0-9562606-6-6).

Gladys runs the Gladys Famoriyo Academy where female authors, speakers and leaders are coached and given expert advice through coaching, seminars, workshops and consultancy services.

Gladys has also recently launched GF Books, a boutique publishing house and consultancy that specialises in self-help, motivational/inspirational, personal development, wellbeing, business and Christian books.

Gladys is also the founder of Gladys Famoriyo Ministries, which oversees a number of initiatives to meet the holistic needs of women. One of such is the *Overcoming Emotional Baggage for Women Initiative* that aims to promote emotional restoration and wellbeing through practical principles and strategies delivered through conferences, retreats, seminars/workshops, and much more. Her latest project is the *Bounce Back Initiative* that helps people flip their challenging life situation on its head, create meaning and purpose out of the experience and positively transform their lives by proactively taking action to help others.

Websites:
www.gladysf.com & www.gladysfministries.com

Connect with Gladys Famoriyo
Follow us | Like us | Engage with us
Facebook/gladysfamoriyo
Facebook/gladysfamoriyoministries
Twitter/gladysfamoriyo
Twitter/gladysfministry
YouTube/GladysFamoriyo
Youtube.com/GladysFamoriyoMinistriesInternational

Also Available from the Author

QUIT HIDING, START LIVING!

How Women Can Free Themselves From Past Hurts

By Gladys Famoriyo

GF Books
ISBN 978-0-9562606-6-6

It is no wonder that we run for cover and put up the barricades when we have been hurt by others. For it seems to be the only way we can protect our sensitive souls and wounded hearts from future hurts.

Well, you know what? That is not the life that God has planned for you. Hiding yourself away from others with a 'no entry' sign on your heart, nursing your wounds and being scared of people who you think might hurt you or are out there to get you, can have a detrimental effect on your physical, emotional and spiritual health. Living in the grip of fear, bitterness, the inability to forgive, anger or resentment is no life for you!

And so, *Quit Hiding, Start Living!* will help you with the following:

- Discover why you might be 'hiding'
- Uncover the hurtful experiences and mental traits that make you susceptible

- Learn how to use a 'retreat' beneficially, and not as a means of escape
- Help you get out there again – with boundaries in place
- Support you in forging healthy relationships – and taking it slow
- Actively deal with 'people issues' as they arrive, so that wounds do not fester
- Learn to forgive and open your heart to God and others

Working through the book and its exercises will allow you to discover and embrace God's plan for you and your valuable and active role in His community.

* * *

'How many women have been hurt, betrayed and abused? The figure is higher than we might care to think about. How many are too ashamed to admit and talk about what has happened? All too often, such women hide their shame, grief and anger inside and try to carry on as usual. All too often the repressed emotional anguish can come out in physical pain and disturbances in bodily function and are treated by drugs with limited success. The fact that unexplained illnesses like Irritable Bowel Syndrome are so much commoner in women than men may represent this hidden hurt.

In *Quit Hiding, Start Living!* Gladys Famoriyo encourages women to open up their hearts, acknowledge what has happened and start living. A dedicated teacher, the compassion and understanding expressed in her book will be an

Also Available from the Author

inspiration for the multitude of women nursing unresolved hurt and shame, often in physical illness.'

Professor Nick Read (Physician and Psychotherapist.
Director of The IBS Network, the national charity for patients
with Irritable Bowel Syndrome www.theibsnetwork.org)
Author of *Sick and Tired, Healing the Illnesses Doctors Cannot Cure.*

* * *

'Quit Hiding, Start Living! *is an insightful read which peers into the recesses of the heart and asks some deep and searching questions about where we find ourselves and how we got there. If you find yourself identifying with the 'hiding woman' syndrome, this book is both therapeutic and inspirational as it encourages healing and the vision to move forward to a more fulfilling life.* Quit Hiding, Start Living! *will encourage positive introspective thinking which is necessary for someone struggling with forgiveness and the inability to overcome hurts. Want a prescription for healing? Read the book and embrace a more abundant life.'*

Sharon Platt-McDonald (Director of Health, Disability & Women Ministries, British Union Conference of The Seventh-day Adventist UK).
Author, *Healing Hearts; Restoring Minds* and *Extending the Olive Branch: Forgiveness as Healing*

* * *

To order, visit www.gladysfministries.com. Both the paperback and ebook versions are also available at book retailers, including online retailers such as Apple iBookstore and Amazon.

HEALING A DISCOURAGED HEART

Getting Back on Track When Life Lets You Down

By Gladys Famoriyo

GF Books
ISBN: 978-0-9562606-3-5

You Prayed. You Hoped. You Waited ...

Yet, life is not turning out the way you planned. And now you are labouring under feelings of abandonment, confusion, disappointment and broken dreams. Deep within you, a crisis of faith brews that throws up questions like: Why me? Where is God? Why is this happening to me? Does He care? When your difficult, uncertain or desperate situation persists, you find yourself becoming weary and discouraged. And the hope that once lit up your heart has all but ebbed away.

So what now?

Author, speaker and coach Gladys Famoriyo knows exactly how you feel. And in her journey to catapult herself out of the chasm of discouragement, she rediscovered some essential lessons about God, life and everything else in between. One crucial lesson was the fact that God hears ... God answers ... just not always the way we are expecting. This can be a hard pill to swallow but one that can bring about inner peace and hope at times when it feels like God has failed to show up as expected.

And so, *Healing a Discouraged Heart* offers practical insights, useful exercises, enlightening human stories and inspiring Bible quotations to offer new perspectives, real hope and an uplifted heart.

* * *

'Healing a Discouraged Heart: Getting Back on Track When Life Let's You Down *is an exceptional read. Powerfully presented with real life scenarios, which the reader can relate to, this insightful and inspirational book will challenge your thinking, deepen your analysis and enable you to question your emotions, behaviors and perceptions when faced with critical life events. Truly an inspired book which speaks to seasons of life, recognises human pain and offers the encouragement that one needs to restore hurting hearts and refocus the mind on God. A true remedy for the soul.*'

Sharon Platt-McDonald (Director of Health, Disability & Women Ministries, British Union Conference of The Seventh-day Adventist UK). Author, *Healing Hearts; Restoring Minds and Extending the Olive Branch: Forgiveness as Healing*

* * *

To order, visit www.gladysfministries.com. Both the paperback and ebook versions are also available at book retailers, including online retailers such as Apple iBookstore and Amazon.

OVERCOMING EMOTIONAL BAGGAGE

A Woman's Guide to Living the Abundant Life

By Gladys Famoriyo

Milestones International Publishers
ISBN 0-924748-73-7

It's Time to Ditch the Baggage!

On our journeys in life, we experience challenges and/or perturbing situations that may result in hurt, pain, disappointment, grief and separation, leaving many of us emotionally battered, bruised and wounded. As a result, many end up accumulating emotional baggage.

Often, our busy and cluttered lives mean we have little or no time to deal with this as there are goals, tasks and busy schedules that must be kept up with.

Hence, we tend to bury our heads in the sand, get back on our treadmills and try our best to get on with life – with our unresolved or unfinished issues in tow. To hide our issues or deal with our inner unrest, we adopt techniques such as wearing masks, comfort eating and retail therapy, though they don't serve us.

Therefore, *Overcoming Emotional Baggage* is the perfect book for women who want to live their lives baggage-free.

Based on biblical principles, this book will support you in uncovering your baggage and empower you to start your journey to wholeness. Filled with useful exercises and practical insights, this book is a valuable resource for individual use as well as in a small group setting.

'I am amazed and delighted. Powerful and much needed information.'
Dr. Wanda A. Davis-Turner – Speaker & Author. USA

'If you have faced disappointments, you will receive strength and support from reading this book. Those involved in ministering to and mentoring women will also find this a useful reference.'
Millicent Brown – Director, Women's Ministries
New Testament Church of God. UK

'Powerful, analytical and definitely life-changing! More than just another self-help book. Soothes the soul, revives the spirit and restores the mind.'

Sharon Platt-McDonald (Director of Health, Disability & Women Ministries, British Union Conference of The Seventh-day Adventist UK). Author, *Healing Hearts; Restoring Minds and Extending the Olive Branch: Forgiveness as Healing*

* * *

To order, visit www.gladysfministries.com. Both the paperback and ebook versions are also available at book retailers, including online retailers such as Apple iBookstore and Amazon.

The Overcoming Emotional Baggage For Women Initiative

The Overcoming Emotional Baggage for Women Initiative is all about offering real hope and fresh perspectives when it comes to dealing with matters of the heart and soul. We do this through our events and programmes including our annual national conference and regional events that includes retreats, seminars and workshops. Our goal is to teach practical, biblical-based principles and strategies to empower women and bring about positive change in their attitudes, beliefs and behaviours that will promote emotional restoration and wellbeing.

We also work with groups and churches, equipping them with tools and information so they can offer support to women in their churches and communities.

Our focus continues to be providing women and young ladies with relevant, practical, easy-to-use yet God-centred information, skills and resources, which they can apply immediately to their lives. Our goal is to see women mature in their faith whilst embracing 'baggage-free', purpose-driven, abundant life.

To find out more, visit www.gladysfministries.com.

Further support

Below are the contact details of some useful organisations that can help you Bounce Back!

Premier Lifeline: The National Christian Helpline
Offering listening ear, emotional and spiritual support and prayer.
Telephone: 0300 11101 01 (UK) – open 9am to midnight everyday
Website: www.premier.org.uk/Premier-Lifeline

Premier Mind and Soul
A Christian response to Mental Health
Website: www.mindandsoul.info

Mental Health Access Pack
Online resource giving insight into the range of subjects relating to Mental Health
Website: www.mentalhealthaccesspack.org

Association of Christian Counsellors
Coordinating body for Christian Counselling
Website: www.acc-uk.org

Mercy Ministries UK
Mercy Ministries UK is a Christian charity that works in partnership with churches across the UK to provide resources, training and residential care for young women who are dealing with life controlling issues.
Website: www.mercyministries.co.uk

Ellel Ministries
A non-denominational Christian ministry that serves the Body of Christ in two main ways – by offering personal prayer ministry to those in need and by training and equipping people so that they can help others more effectively.
Telephone: Glyndley Manor Centre: 44 (0) 1323 440440
Website: www.ellel.org/uk

Christians Against Poverty
Debt counselling charity that is passionate about lifting people out of debt and poverty through their award winning debt help service and money management course, the CAP Money Course.
Telephone: 44 (0) 1274 760720
Website: www.capuk.org

The Mariposa Trust & Saying Goodbye
Helping people who have been affected by the loss of a child at any stage of pregnancy, at birth or in infancy.

Offers befriending, support, information and international remembrance services for people who have lost a child.
Websites: www.mariposatrust.org & www.sayinggoodbye.org
Telephone: +44 (0) 845 293 8028 / (0) 845 293 8027

Gift of Living Donation (G.O.L.D.)
Promotes living kidney donation and raises awareness of organ donation especially within the African and Caribbean community living in the UK.
Telephone: +44 (0) 020 8451 1605
Website: www.morethanamatch.co.uk

Women's Aid
A national charity for women and children working to end domestic abuse.
Telephone: 0808 2000 (UK) - 24-hour national domestic violence helpline
Website: www.womensaid.org.uk

Prospects
Christian organisation working in the area of learning disability.
Website: www.prospects.org.uk

Churches for All
Campaign for a Church that fully enables everyone to play their part whatever their ability or disability.
Website: www.churchesforall.org.uk

My Notes

My Notes

My Notes

GF
BOOKS

Changing lives through words
www.gladysfbooks.com